East
Meets
Vegan

East Meets Vegan

The Best of Asian Home Cooking,
Plant-Based and Delicious

Sasha Gill

THE EXPERIMENT

NEW YORK

India ²⁷

Thailand ⁶⁹

Singapore ¹⁰¹
& Malaysia

China

Japan

Introduction

I grew up in the kitchen. Some of my earliest memories revolve around helping my mother make pineapple tarts. *Hands off the pineapple jam!* Or flipping through my nana's handwritten recipes, the pages stained with little bits of butter – mementos of the curries they helped to create. I loved helping around the kitchen. Not because, at the age of seven, I was terribly interested in the cooking itself; it was more about what I could sneak a taste of when no one was looking. My sister and I used to have a deal: She would get to lick the bowl clean, while I got the balloon whisk, its crevices hiding little pockets of cake batter. Cooking – and eating – is the one thing my family loved to do, and we do it well.

I moved from Singapore to the UK for secondary school, convinced I wouldn't miss home. I was so excited to jump headfirst into my new life in a country with a cold climate and soft grey skies (in hindsight, creature of habit that I am, such a change must surely have terrified me). I lasted two weeks before I missed home, my family, proper sunshine, and my favorite *popiah* spring rolls. When the summer holidays finally rolled around, I returned and stuffed myself silly with popiah: juicy, stewed jicama encased in paper-thin crêpes, studded with roasted peanuts. *How I had missed it!*

Nowadays, studying medicine at Oxford University, I spend my time trying to master the art of getting out of bed by seven in the morning (I am not quite there yet), and pushing the boundaries of how long I can leave a bike unlocked without it getting stolen (hint: don't). The kitchen, however small and lackluster it may be, is and will remain my happy place. Clichés aside, cooking is my escape. When life is a whirlwind of activity that sets my head spinning, cooking grounds me. And life, as we all know, is often a whirlwind.

I had toyed with the idea of vegetarianism many times before, but always had an excuse not to take the leap. Until one day, none of those excuses seemed good enough anymore. When I was seventeen, I decided to stop eating meat. A few months later, I stopped eating animal products altogether. Going vegan wasn't as hard as I had imagined, although my decision was met with a copious number of questions. *So, what do you eat? Don't you need protein? Doesn't it get boring just eating salad? Don't you miss it?*

Deep down, I *did* miss it. I missed my favorite tandoori chicken and my grandfather's famous sugee cake. I missed being able to eat all the things I used to love. It wasn't the meat or the eggs and dairy that I craved, but the *flavor*.

As I got better at cooking plant foods I realized that the deep flavors I missed so much did not have to come from animal products. I made alternative versions of family recipes, one by one, trying to keep everything as authentic as possible. These were not lesser versions of their non-plant counterparts, or something only I enjoyed. They had a spot in the center of the dinner table, so that everyone – plant-eater and carnivore alike – could help themselves.

Singapore, which I still call home, is a melting pot of cultures, and with this comes an extraordinary array of food. As a greeting, you get asked, "Are you hungry?" before anything else. With people drawn from all across Asia and beyond, food is our universal language. I feel lucky to have been surrounded by such a wonderful, diverse food scene for so much of my life. That is why I decided to write this book. I want everyone to be able to enjoy the amazing food Asia has to offer, in their own homes. And, *hey*, it just so happens to be plant-based, too! With all the incredible spices and sauces, you don't miss anything. *Not at all.*

Some may be intimidated by Asian cooking. The variety of Indian spices can dazzle even the bravest home cook, and it might be difficult trying to wrap your head around ingredients with foreign names. This book is here to help you. As a university student, I get that spending too much time and money cooking can be a worry. Trust me, *I do.* The recipes in this book are all designed to be accessible, affordable and easy to whip up. So, whether it's a snappy Monday packed lunch or a Friday evening get-together, you'll find a recipe perfect for the occasion.

Most importantly, this book isn't about restriction. Rather, it is a celebration of abundance, a celebration of plant foods and all the amazing things they can do.

So what do I eat? I eat plants. And they are pretty awesome.

Recipe notes

Before starting a recipe, read it through at least once so you have a general idea of what to do. I also like to have everything measured out in little bowls before I start, just to make things easier.

All measurements in this book are as follows:

1 tablespoon = 20 ml
1 teaspoon = 5 ml
1 cup = 250 ml

If the way an ingredient should be prepared is given before the ingredient's name, measure it only after prepping it. If the preparation appears after the name, measure the ingredient whole, then chop, grind, mince or sift as appropriate. This affects the weight of the ingredient you are using, so it's important! For example: "1 cup sifted flour" is 120 g, and is measured after the flour is sifted into a bowl; "1 cup flour, sifted" or just "1 cup flour" is 150 g, and is scooped from the package straight into the measuring cup, and then sifted into a bowl with the other ingredients.

All ginger, garlic, shallots and onions called for are peeled before use. Shallots are red Asian shallots, unless specified.

All sugars and syrups can be swapped, except in the baking recipes. When baking, syrups are interchangeable (e.g., you can swap rice syrup for maple syrup) but not dry sugars.

All "vegetable oil" is interchangeable in these recipes – try to use a neutral-flavored oil. But if sesame oil, coconut oil or vegan butter is explicitly called for, do not substitute it.

All plant milks used are interchangeable, unless a specific milk is stipulated in the recipe.

 GF indicates that a recipe is, or can be made, gluten-free.

 This spicy symbol indicates a chili-hot dish – see page 16 for a note on heat levels and how to adjust them to your own taste and tolerance.

Pantry essentials

I like to keep a well-stocked pantry, so that if I am ever busy, or running late, I save myself a trip to the shops. If you are just building up your own pantry, start small. Buy new ingredients as you need them, and soon enough you will have built up your own repertoire of aromatic spices and multicolored purees. Asian cooking calls for many different pastes, spices and other little bits, which can often be overwhelming. Here is a list of some of the more niche ingredients used in this book, where to find them, or how to substitute them if you can't get them where you live. A general rule of thumb in your search for some of these ingredients (as with most things you will ever need to buy) is that you can almost always find them online.

— Agar powder

This is a great vegetarian alternative to gelatin, and is often found in the West as a powder or as flakes. In Asia, you can also get it in strips. I use powdered agar in this book, and it is the one I recommend you get, as it is the easiest to work with! Unlike gelatin, it must be boiled for at least 5 minutes to make sure it sets properly into a jelly.

— Agave or rice syrup

Some of the recipes call for a liquid sweetener, and I usually use agave or rice syrup, as they lend a lovely caramel note to your cooking. You should be able to find them in most supermarkets, either in the baking aisle or the sugar aisle.

— Aquafaba

This ingredient is perhaps the most elusive in the book. It is not a weird Asian ingredient at all, but something almost everyone will have sitting in their pantry at this very moment. Aquafaba means "bean water," and it is the slightly viscous liquid that you find in a tin of chickpeas. It is an excellent egg substitute in baking, and I adore cooking with it. In fact, you can use the liquid from pretty much any type of bean, although I do suggest using a white bean so it doesn't affect the color of the final dish too much. Whenever I open a can of beans, I drain the aquafaba into ice-cube trays and pop them in the freezer. If you make each cube with 1 or 2 tablespoons, you'll know how much to take out and melt when you need to use some aquafaba in your baking.

— Beans

Whether canned or dried, beans are also little protein powerhouses, and I love using them. I cook with canned versions if I can find them, as they are a lot easier and don't require as much pre-planning. But if you own a pressure cooker and so can cook dried beans quite quickly, you may prefer to use them. You can also pop dried beans in some water in a slow cooker in the morning, go about your day and then have them ready by dinnertime. I also use some beans you may be less familiar with, such as adzuki beans and mung beans. Adzuki beans are small, maroon beans that are commonly cooked down in sugar, then mashed and used in Japanese desserts. Mung beans are common in Southeast Asian cooking, both in savory and sweet dishes. Look for them in the whole foods sections of supermarkets – and if you live near a health-food store, you might find some in the bulk bins, and they may well be cheaper, too.

— Black salt

Black salt (*kala namak*) is, shockingly, not black, but rather pinkish and high in sulfur, with a whiff of egg to it. So, perhaps unsurprisingly, black salt is often used in vegan cooking to impart an egg-like flavor and aroma to your dishes. I love cooking with kala namak and sometimes use it instead of regular salt, just to add a little more complexity. If possible, try to add it toward the end of cooking, as this retains more of its eggy flavor. Black salt is becoming increasingly easy to find in supermarkets, but otherwise you should be able to track it down online. It is one of my favorite ingredients, and I do recommend you give it a try.

— Chickpea flour

Chickpea flour, also referred to as besan or gram flour, is often used in Indian snacks and desserts. Because it is high in protein and gluten-free, it is increasing in popularity around the world and makes an incredible plant-based omelet! You should be able to find it in most supermarkets and health-food stores, or online.

— Cooking wines

Chinese and Japanese cooking wines – Shaoxing and mirin – are both rice wines. If you cannot find either, a dry sherry can be used. And if you avoid alcohol, you can substitute it with apple juice.

— Galangal

A common ingredient in Thai and Malaysian cooking, galangal is ginger's sharper, more citrusy cousin, and is often referred to as "blue ginger" in Asia. It can be found in fresh or paste form, and I like to use the latter since it stores well and is easier to work with – galangal is much tougher than ginger and can be hard to grate. Look for it in Asian grocery stores, but if you have no luck, just use the same amount of ginger – and, if possible, add a small spoonful of lime juice to mimic the acidity that galangal would impart.

— Makrut lime leaves

Another star ingredient of Thai cooking, these leaves are added to soups or broths to give them a lovely citrus note. The dried version can be found in most supermarkets in the spice aisle. The fresh ones are a gorgeous deep green color with a beautiful gloss to them, but you may have to hunt more for these. If you can't find either, use a bay leaf and a squeeze of lime juice instead.

— *Kecap manis*

This sweet soy sauce is used in a lot of Indonesian and Malaysian cooking. It is thick and syrupy, with an almost treacle-like flavor. It is extremely versatile and can be used to flavor rice, stir-fries, marinades and so on. You can find kecap manis in many supermarkets, sometimes labeled as sweet soy sauce. If you are having trouble finding it, there's a recipe for making your own on page 21.

— Lemongrass

Lemongrass is prominent in Thai cooking, and you might be familiar with its calming aroma from scented candles and massage oils. You should be able to find fresh and pureed lemongrass in most supermarkets, but in a pinch, lemon zest will provide some of its effervescence.

— Lentils

Oh, lentils. I *live* off them. They are easy to cook, store well in your kitchen cupboards, and pack some good plant-based protein into your diet. Indian cooking uses a variety of lentils, the most common of which is the red split lentil, core ingredient of *tarka dal*. *Urad dal*, also called black gram, is the lentil called for in *dal makhani*, and when making dosas. These are the two lentils called for in this book, although I do encourage you to try a whole lot more and experiment with their different flavors and textures. Red split lentils are readily available at any supermarket, but urad dal is a little harder to find – I get mine from an Indian grocery store, and it is also available online.

— Miso

Miso is a fermented paste used in Japanese cooking, usually made from soy beans, a culture, salt and a grain. It adds a gorgeous, savory umami kick. Other countries have their own versions: Korea has *doenjang*, while Malaysia has *tauco*. I use miso paste interchangeably for these, as they all have similar flavors and miso is the easiest to find. White miso has a shorter ferment and an almost buttery flavor, while dark miso is more aged, with a deeper, more complex flavor. I use dark miso in all my cooking, as it is the one I prefer, but you can also use white miso whenever it is called for in this book. As it is mostly made with barley, miso is not typically gluten-free. If you're looking for a gluten-free alternative, keep an eye out for brown rice miso. While you can find miso in almost any supermarket, if you're looking for the gluten-free sort, a health-food store will probably be your best bet.

— **Oyster sauce**

Interestingly, this is one of the easiest ingredients to find a vegetarian substitute for, as the company that first made oyster sauce now makes a vegetarian version as well. It is often sold as "vegetarian oyster sauce" in Asia, but it may also be called "vegetarian stir-fry sauce" or "mushroom sauce." The brand you are looking for is Lee Kum Kee, and you should be able to find it at most major supermarkets. If all else fails, just fry some mushrooms and keep the liquid they release as they cook, then use this in place of oyster sauce, adding a pinch of sugar as well.

— **Palm sugar**

Palm sugar is often used in Malaysian and Singaporean cooking, where it is referred to as *gula Melaka*, and in India, where it is called jaggery. Either way, it is a brownish, natural sugar often sold in a block form, with a deep caramelized taste. You can find the granulated form in most supermarkets, although often sold in very small portions. I suggest buying your palm sugar at an international supermarket, where you can get better value, or using coconut sugar instead, as it has a similarly complex, roasted flavor. Dark brown sugar can also be used.

— **Pandan**

Pandan is the flavor of my childhood. At teatime, we would sometimes get a pandan chiffon cake to share – a light and cloud-like treat, and a beautiful hue of pastel green. Pandan is to Southeast Asia what vanilla is to the West. It flavors our puddings, adds mellow coconut-like notes to our rice. Its elusive fragrance is like a blend of coconut, vanilla and licorice. Pandan is commonly sold as leaves or extract. I like to use the leaves, for a more natural flavor and color; the extract will also dye your food a vibrant green, which may not be ideal in all dishes! Look for pandan leaves or extract in Thai or other Southeast Asian supermarkets. Leaves are also sold frozen, as they last a lot longer while keeping their amazing floral qualities. If you cannot find pandan anywhere, vanilla can be substituted to approximate it in sweet dishes, while bay leaves can be used in savory.

— **Rice and rice flour**

Someone once told me that I ate too much rice. But for me, a meal just doesn't feel complete without it! In this book, I use a variety of rice: basmati for Indian cooking, jasmine for Thai and Malaysian food, sushi rice for Japanese cooking, and glutinous rice for desserts. While you might be tempted to buy just one type of rice for all these recipes, hear me out on this one. Each grain is different. Basmati is a slender, long-grain rice that is drier and has a nutty flavor, making it a perfect bed for thick gravies and rich curries. Jasmine is also a long-grain rice, but that's where the similarities end. Jasmine has a coconutty, pandan-like taste, and it pairs beautifully with the aromatics of Malaysian and Thai cooking. Sushi rice is a short-grain rice and is a lot more starchy than the previous two. It becomes sticky when cooked, and this allows it to be shaped for sushi, typically seasoned with vinegar and sugar. Lastly, glutinous rice (also called sticky rice, sweet rice or mochi rice) is also a short-grain rice that's commonly used for sweet dishes – despite the name, it's completely gluten-free. Unlike most rice, it is almost always cooked in a steamer, and this means it retains its bite. It is commonly used in puddings. You should find the first three types of rice at your local supermarket, but sticky rice may prove a bit trickier – check online or in Asian grocery stores. Glutinous rice flour is also used in the book; you should be able to find it online or at a Chinese supermarket.

WHAT ABOUT LEFTOVER RICE?

In Asia, recooking leftover rice is pretty common. I used to do it all the time. But when I first came to the UK, I realized that cooked rice needs to be treated with caution, because it can give you a bad case of food poisoning. I hate wasting food and if, like me, you always cook more than you need, you could end up with lots of leftover rice. Always cool the rice as soon as possible and never leave it at room temperature for too long. As a rough guide, I try to refrigerate any leftover rice within an hour of cooking. When recooking it, you always need to make sure it is heated thoroughly all the way through by cooking it in a hot wok or pan and checking that everything is piping hot before serving. Never reheat rice more than once.

— Seaweed

Seaweed was my favorite snack at primary school. I ate it daily in my school canteen: little sheets roasted in sesame oil and heavily salted. They had a flavor akin to kale chips, with a hint of the ocean. Nowadays, my seaweed obsession has manifested in a different form. I have, in my pantry, a rather impressive collection of seaweeds, from kelp and wakame to the more regular nori sheets for sushi. While you by no means have to acquire a comparable collection, I do recommend finding some nori for your cooking. It can be used in soups and broths, to add a fishy flavor, and for rolling sushi and wrapping onigiri. You should be able to find it in the world food aisle of most supermarkets, or online, of course. Once open, store in a ziplock bag in the fridge, as this helps it last much longer. Especially since – contrary to what my eight-year-old self would argue – seaweed isn't something you cook with every day.

— Shiitake mushrooms

This robust, meaty mushroom imparts a wonderful, deep flavor to any soup or stock. You can get them fresh or dried; I prefer to buy the dried version as they last a long time. If you have a local Asian grocer, look there first – they'll probably be cheaper than the supermarket.

— Soy sauce

Dark soy sauce is richer and more syrupy than light soy sauce. It is helpful to have both in your pantry, as they aren't as interchangeable as they sound. In a pinch, you can use light for dark, but the color of the final dish will be affected.

— Spices

Now, let's talk about spices. There are so many of them! I can't resist spices and have built up quite a collection: from vibrant-green cardamom pods, with notes of eucalyptus, to elusive asafetida – so pungent that the spice bottle is encased in its own airtight box. Ground spices will generally last for around nine months in an opened bottle, while whole spices last a lot longer, up to two years. After that, they start to lose flavor and won't be as vivid. Some swear by grinding their own spices; while I agree that freshly ground cinnamon is beautifully rich and aromatic, grinding spices can be time consuming. This is by no means an exhaustive list of Asian spices and spice blends, but these are the ones I use often. If you are just starting out on your own spice collection, get the essentials first: Those listed in bold are the foundations of Asian cooking.

Asafoetida
Bay leaves
Cardamom (ground and pods)
Cayenne pepper
Chili powder
Cinnamon (ground and sticks)
Cloves
Coriander (ground and seeds)
Cumin (ground and seeds)
Curry leaves
Curry powder – mild
Dried chilies
Fenugreek seeds and leaves
Five spice powder
Garam masala
Ginger (ground)
Mustard seeds
Nutmeg
Saffron
Star anise
Turmeric (ground)

A NOTE ON HEAT

I once won a chili-eating competition. The challenge was to eat as many chilies as you could before you gave up and downed a glass of milk. I ate twenty-five chilies, and technically I'm still going, since I never had that glass of milk! The point is, I can eat *a lot* of chili. However, I get that not everyone likes such fiery food. If you aren't too good with spice, you can always cut back on the chili to bring it down a notch. For any recipe calling for fresh chili, you can use less or just remove all the seeds. The seeds are usually where most of the heat is; however, bird's eye chilies are still spicy without their seeds, so just use fewer of them. If dried chili or chili powder is called for, use half the amount or cut it out entirely.

— Spring roll wrappers

There are two types of spring roll wrappers you can buy. The first is made primarily of rice flour, is translucent, and must be soaked briefly in water to soften it. The other is made with wheat flour, is opaque, and can often be found in the freezer section under the name "spring roll pastry." Both types of wrappers are used in this book, so try to use the one that is called for. For a gluten-free option, however, you can use the softened rice wrappers instead of the wheat kind. Contrary to what it might say on the packet, the rice wrappers only need to be dunked in water for 2–4 seconds, and will soften a little more as you lay the filling out on them.

— Tamarind paste

This tangy, slightly sweet pulp is used in India, Thailand, Malaysia and Singapore to add acidity. I like to use the paste as it is easy to work with, but if you can only find it in block form, tear off a chunk, soak it in a little hot water for about 5 minutes and then strain the pulp to remove the seeds. You can usually find tamarind paste in supermarkets, but if not, you can substitute it with twice the amount of lime or lemon juice and a pinch of brown sugar.

Equipment

I like to collect things, kitchen appliances being one of them. However, as a university student, I often need to pack up everything I own. And so having too large a collection can start to get a bit problematic. Here are some of the kitchen essentials I could not live without, plus a couple of bonus items if you feel like treating yourself!

Essentials

— Blender

A blender is best for making soup, lassi and other drinks. Stick to blending soft ingredients, unless you own a high-speed blender – they can even crush ice or harder whole vegetables, such as carrots.

— Food processor

Food processors, on the other hand, are great at crushing harder ingredients, and can also be used to roughly chop your onions and garlic, not to mention making curry pastes.

— Knives

Contrary to what you might think, a good, sharp knife can prevent you from injuring yourself. It's more likely to slice through what you are cutting than to run down the sides of it and hit your hand. Of course, injuries can still happen, but keeping your knife razor-sharp while remaining cautious can minimize kitchen-related mishaps. If you're looking for a good all-purpose knife, get a chef's knife. If you are willing to get several knives, a paring knife and a serrated knife make good additions to your collection. I also recommend using a knife sharpener at least once a month, or whenever you notice the blade is getting dull.

— Nonstick frying pan

I swear by my nonstick frying pan. I don't like to cook with too much oil, as I am incredibly clumsy and always manage to burn myself with oil splatters (my stove has a questionable thermostat). A nonstick pan is just what you need, for anything from crispy dosas to pineapple fried rice. If you haven't already got one, my advice is to shell out a bit more money when buying it, as quality really matters here. Cheaper nonstick pans can lose their nonstick coating after one or two uses. I prefer ceramic pans to PTFE-coated pans, as it is safer for you and better for the environment. It's essential that you take good care of your pan so that it lasts a long time. When cooking with it, try to avoid using too high a heat as this can degrade nonstick coating, and use wooden or silicone spatulas rather than metal utensils. When washing up your pan, let it cool completely first, then use a lot of warm, soapy water and a soft sponge. Metal scourers or brushes with plastic bristles can scratch the coating. Avoid placing in the dishwasher, as the high heat can reduce the pan's life span, even if it claims to be dishwasher-safe.

— Steamer basket

This may seem like an odd one to include on a list of kitchen essentials. But as this is a cookbook for Asian cooking, a steamer basket is pretty much one of the most important kitchen tools. In Asia, so many things are steamed, from plain vegetables to lovely stuffed buns and dumplings. I use a bamboo steamer that's the same diameter as my saucepan, and line it with parchment paper. You can also get a metal steamer insert, which folds up and so is a lot more compact to store.

Extras

— Microplane

It's hard to imagine life without a Microplane – if you own one, you'll know what I mean! These are incredible for turning lemon peel into a fine citrusy zest, transforming ginger into a pulp and even for grinding cinnamon straight from the stick! Whenever I call for very finely chopped ginger, garlic or lemongrass in this book, my Microplane is what I use. If you don't want to get one just yet, use a fine grater instead, or just spend some time chopping with a knife.

— Mortar and pestle

I use my mortar and pestle to make curry pastes, to grind whole spices or toasted rice into a powder and to crush peanuts or palm sugar. You should definitely consider getting a mortar and pestle if you cook a lot of Thai food, as a curry paste made this way is much silkier and more flavorful than one made in a food processor. If a recipe calls for a mortar and pestle, such as Green papaya salad (page 70), but you do not have one, just use a large sturdy bowl and a blunt instrument, like the end of a rolling pin, to pound down into the bowl.

— Rolling pin

Rolling pins are great for getting homemade dumpling skins whisper-thin and even. You don't need a fancy one with revolving handles; I just use a simple wooden one. You can also improvise: An old balsamic vinegar bottle was my rolling pin for a good two years before I got a proper one.

— Silicone mat

I love my silicone mat. I use it to line my baking sheet whenever I use it. It's wonderfully nonstick, completely reusable and a breeze to clean –everything just slides off! As someone who bakes a lot, I love using this instead of parchment paper as it's more environmentally friendly, and you'll make back the money you spend on it over the long term.

— Tofu press

Pressing tofu isn't something you should ever skip when using it in a dish. You can now get tofu presses online that make pressing tofu a breeze! If space isn't too much of a problem for you, and you want to save time, by all means look into getting one. Alternatively, you can press tofu as described on page 25.

— Wok

Stir-frying is just so much easier in a wok: There is a larger surface area to toss the food on, and it is less likely to spill over the edge of the pan and make a mess. Pad thai can be difficult to clean off your stove! At home, we use an old, heavy cast-iron wok, but if you are thinking of getting one, just remember that it needs a lot of care and upkeep. Nonstick or stainless-steel woks are also good choices.

Basic recipes and techniques

As you cook your way through the fragrant curries, piquant soups and fruity desserts in this book, you may come across an ingredient that can be made at home. Although you can, of course, use store-bought versions if you prefer – here are some basic recipes and techniques you might want to have a go at yourself.

Basic recipes

Burmese tofu

Makes about 20 ounces (600 g), roughly equivalent to 2 blocks of tofu

—

½ cup (60 g) chickpea flour
pinch of ground turmeric
½ teaspoon salt

This is a great substitute for the tofu in savory recipes if you avoid soy products. Lightly oil a loaf pan and line with parchment paper. In a bowl or blender, mix the flour, turmeric, salt and 1½ cups (375 ml) water into a smooth batter. Pour the batter into a saucepan and bring to a boil, stirring constantly. Reduce the heat to as low as possible and cook for a further 3–5 minutes, still stirring constantly, until thick and glossy, with a similar consistency to choux pastry. Scrape into the pan and smooth the top as best you can. Transfer to the fridge and leave to set for at least an hour, then take out of the pan and cut into cubes. Store in an airtight container in the fridge for up to 4 days.

Chicken-style seasoning

Makes about ¼ cup (75 g)

—

¼ cup plus 1 tablespoon (20 g) nutritional yeast
1 teaspoon celery salt (or regular salt)
½ teaspoon dried sage
pinch of dried oregano
pinch of sweet smoked paprika

Place all the ingredients in a food processor or bullet blender and process until fine and powderlike. Store in a small jar in a cool place, as you would for a spice.

Chili oil

Makes about ¼ cup (60 ml)

—

¼ cup plus 1 tablespoon (80 ml) oil
2 large chilies, seeds removed, very finely chopped

This chili oil results in beautiful, amber speckles in whatever broth it is added to. This version is not too spicy, but if you prefer more of a kick, leave in a few chili seeds. Pour the oil into a small saucepan and set over medium heat. Add the chili and fry for 5–7 minutes, stirring constantly to prevent burning. When ready, the oil should have turned slightly orange from the chili. Remove from the heat, strain out the chili, then store the oil in a small jar in a cool, dark place for up to 3 weeks.

Compressed rice

Serves 4

—

1½ cups (300 g) jasmine rice
1 pandan leaf, knotted (or 1 bay leaf)
¼ teaspoon salt

Place the rice, pandan leaf and salt in a saucepan with 3 cups (750 ml) water and bring to a boil. Reduce to a simmer, cover the pan and cook for about 15 minutes until the rice is tender, stirring every now and then.

Tear off a sheet of foil measuring about 20 x 12 inches (50 x 30 cm) and grease it. Use the foil to line an 8-inch (20 cm) square brownie pan, with the greased side facing up, letting the excess hang foil over the sides.

When the rice has had its 15 minutes, remove the pandan leaf. Use a potato masher to mash the rice, and continue to cook it until all the water has evaporated. Pour the mashed rice into the prepared pan, smoothing it out into an even layer, then fold the excess foil over to cover it completely and press down. Set another brownie pan or other similar-sized baking pan (or improvise with a piece of cardboard cut to fit, covered with foil and greased) on top, and place something heavy on top of that — I use my mortar and pestle — to weigh it down and compress the rice. Leave it to cool for 1–2 hours, then remove the rice from the tray and slice into squares or diamonds.

Dashi

Makes about 1½ cups (375 ml)

—

2 cups (500 ml) vegetable stock
2 dried shiitake mushrooms
½ sheet nori

In a large saucepan over medium heat, bring the vegetable stock, dried mushrooms and nori to a boil. Lower the heat, cover and simmer for 10–15 minutes to let the flavors infuse the stock, then strain, discarding the solids.

Dumpling skins

Makes about 30

—

2 cups (240 g) sifted all-purpose flour
½ teaspoon salt
cornstarch, for dusting

Put the flour and salt in a large bowl, add ⅔ cup (170 ml) water and mix with a wooden spoon until it starts to come together. Turn out and knead by hand for 5–10 minutes, until you have a smooth, elastic ball of dough – if the dough seems too sticky and soft, sprinkle with a little more flour and knead it in. Put the dough back in the bowl, cover with plastic wrap and leave it to rest for 30 minutes at room temperature.

Take a golfball-sized piece of dough and put on a cornstarch-dusted surface. Use a rolling pin to roll out into a circle about 3 mm thick. Use a circular cutter or the rim of a mug to trim it into a perfect circle about 3 inches (7.5 cm) in diameter, returning the dough off-cuts to the bowl. Repeat until you have no more dough left. Stack the dumpling skins on a plate, dusting well with cornstarch to stop them from sticking to each other. You can also interleave them with plastic wrap or parchment paper to keep them from sticking. Cover the whole stack with plastic wrap to prevent the dumpling skins from drying out. If you aren't going to be using them immediately, keep them in the freezer for up to 2 months. (Before using, let the wrappers thaw completely: about 1 hour at room temperature, longer in the fridge.)

Flax egg

Makes the equivalent of 1 egg

—

1 tablespoon plus 1 teaspoon ground flaxseed (or ground chia seeds)

Mix the flax with ¼ cup (60 ml) water in a cup. Set aside until thick and viscous, about 5–10 minutes, before adding to your recipe.

Kecap manis

Makes about ¾ cup (185 ml)

—

½ cup (125 ml) soy sauce
½ cup (100 g) lightly packed dark brown sugar
1 inch (2.5 cm) ginger – optional
2 garlic cloves, crushed – optional

Put all the ingredients in a saucepan over medium heat. Bring to a boil, stirring occasionally, then lower the heat and simmer for 10–15 minutes, until all the sugar is dissolved and the mixture is syrupy. Pour into a sterilized glass jar, discarding the ginger and garlic, then store in the fridge. It will thicken further as it cools.

"Kewpie" mayo

Makes about 1 cup (235 g)

—

¼ cup (60 ml) aquafaba (see page 11), chilled
¼ teaspoon Dijon mustard
½ teaspoon black salt
1 tablespoon rice vinegar or apple cider vinegar
½ teaspoon lemon juice
1 tablespoon plus 1 teaspoon rice syrup
¾ cup (185 ml) vegetable oil, chilled
¼ teaspoon xanthan gum – optional (see below)

Japanese-style mayo is sweeter and more mellow than regular mayonnaise. This vegan version works best when both the aquafaba and oil are cold, as this helps them to emulsify easily.

Place all the ingredients except the oil and xanthan gum in a food processor and blend for 30 seconds to mix them well. With the processor running on high speed, drizzle in the oil in a very slow, thin and steady stream. As you do this, the mixture should thicken to the consistency of mayonnaise. If the mixture does not thicken, your ingredients might not have been cold enough, or your aquafaba could have been too thin to begin with. The good news is that there's an easy fix: Just add ¼ teaspoon xanthan gum (in the specialty flour section of most large supermarkets), blend again and it should thicken immediately.

Store the mayo in a clean glass jar in the fridge for up to 2 weeks.

Red bean paste

Makes about 1½ cups (375 g)

—

½ cup (100 g) dried adzuki beans
¼ cup (55 g) white sugar

Soak the adzuki beans for 4 hours, or overnight. Drain and transfer into a saucepan, then add 1½ cups (375 ml) water and boil for 1 hour or until soft. Remove from the heat and mash well with a potato masher, then add the sugar. Return to medium heat and cook, stirring constantly, until it thickens and no liquid remains – it is done when you can see the bottom of the pan for at least 1 second when you scrape your spatula across it, before the mixture flows back over it. The paste will thicken further as it cools. Store your red bean paste (anko) in a sterilized jar in the fridge for up to a week.

Roasted chickpeas

Makes about 1½ cups (250 g)

—

one 15-ounce (425 g) can
  chickpeas, drained

You can usually buy "toasted chana" in Indian grocery stores, but you can also make your own. Preheat the oven to 400°F (200°C) and line a baking sheet with parchment paper. Pat the chickpeas dry with paper towels to remove as much of the moisture as possible, then spread them out in an even layer on the sheet. Bake for 30 minutes, stirring every 10 minutes, until crisp. Let the roasted chickpeas cool completely before storing in an airtight jar.

Seitan "chicken"

Makes the equivalent of 2 chicken fillets – enough to serve 4

—

1 cup (250 ml) vegetable stock
½ cup (85 g) cooked butter beans
¼ cup plus 1 tablespoon (20 g)
  nutritional yeast
4 garlic cloves
2 teaspoons Chicken-style seasoning
  (page 20), or more yeast
1 teaspoon onion powder
1 tablespoon plus 1 teaspoon tahini
¼ teaspoon ground cumin
½ teaspoon salt – leave out if your
  vegetable stock is salty enough
1 cup (110 g) vital wheat gluten

If your seitan "chicken" is destined for Hainanese "chicken" rice (page 118), add a teaspoon of five spice powder to the dough before kneading for extra flavor.

In a food processor, blend all the ingredients except the vital wheat gluten until smooth. Pour into a large bowl and sift in the wheat gluten. Stir well with a wooden spoon until a wet dough forms. Continue to mix and knead for 5–7 minutes, stretching the dough out and then rolling it back into a ball with each knead. It is ready when the dough appears less wet, has defined strands and bounces back when stretched. The longer you knead the dough, the chewier your seitan will be, so if you prefer things with a good chew to them, knead for an extra 5 minutes.

Set a steamer basket over a pan of boiling water. Cut out 2 large squares of foil and grease them lightly. Place half the dough onto each piece of foil and shape into a log, wrapping the foil around it like a candy wrapper, sealing it well. Steam the seitan logs for 30 minutes, then remove and leave to cool for 30 minutes before refrigerating. The seitan "chicken" will last for up to a week in the fridge.

Serundeng

Makes 1 cup (about 150 g)

—

1 teaspoon coriander seeds
5 shallots, roughly chopped
2 garlic cloves, roughly chopped
1 teaspoon tamarind paste
2½ tablespoons gula Melaka or
  brown sugar
½ teaspoon salt
1 cup (80 g) freshly grated
  coconut
1 inch (2.5 cm) ginger, bruised
1 lemongrass stalk, bruised

As well as being an important ingredient in some of the recipes in this book, this is also a great thing to add to a plate of Nasi lemak (page 115) or to serve as a side with a curry. Ideally, use grated fresh coconut instead of the desiccated kind for this. (If you do end up using desiccated coconut, you'll need the same amount – but it won't need to be toasted for as long, so keep an eye on it!)

First, grind the coriander seeds, shallots, garlic, tamarind, sugar and salt together into a paste, either with a mortar and pestle or food processor. Scrape the paste into a large nonstick frying pan over medium heat and add the coconut. Throw in the ginger and lemongrass and stir-fry until the coconut starts to brown and the mixture looks dry. Store in a sterilized jar in the fridge for up to a week.

Basic techniques

— Preparing TVP granules and chunks

Soak TVP granules in an equivalent volume of hot water for 5–10 minutes, until they have softened. Soak TVP chunks in four times their volume of hot water for about 20 minutes or until it has softened. Before using the soaked TVP granules or chunks in your dish, you'll need to drain it well. You can do this with granules by placing a spoonful at a time of the soaked granules in a sieve and pressing down with the back of a spoon to squeeze out excess water before scooping the now-dry TVP into a clean bowl. For TVP chunks, you can simply squeeze the chunks between your fingers to remove excess water.

— Pressing tofu

Wrap your block of tofu in a clean, lint-free kitchen towel and place a chopping board on top of it. Weigh the board down with something heavy, like a big can of beans, to apply pressure to it. Leave for at least 30 minutes, to press out as much liquid as possible.

— Freezing tofu

If you are struggling to enjoy the texture of tofu, freezing extra-firm tofu – instead of pressing it – transforms it into something that is a lot chewier and even more sponge-like. All you have to do is drain a block (14 ounces/400 g) extra-firm tofu, cut it into cubes or slices, pop in a container and freeze overnight, until completely frozen. When you want to use the tofu in a recipe, thaw it at room temperature for 2–3 hours, then use your hands to wring out all the excess moisture … Quite a lot of liquid should come out of it! This is a lot sturdier than tofu that hasn't been in the freezer, so you don't need to worry too much about it crumbling as you squeeze.

— Preparing jackfruit

After draining your can of young green jackfruit, rinse it well in a sieve under cold running water – this helps to get rid of the slightly sweet jackfruit flavor. After rinsing, cut away the tough core of each piece of jackfruit, then shred the remaining flesh into something resembling pulled pork. Discard all the seeds and seed pods.

— Roasting nuts and seeds

Preheat the oven to 350°F (175°C). Place about 1 cup (140 g) of the nuts you want to roast on a baking sheet and roast for 10–15 minutes, stirring every 5 minutes. Keep an eye on them as some may brown faster than the others.

— Toasting seeds

If you are toasting sesame seeds, this is best done in a nonstick frying pan over medium heat. Dry-fry them until they start to turn golden, about 3–5 minutes, stirring occasionally.

01
India

There is much more to India than curry. Food here is, in fact, wonderfully diverse, taking in everything from the *thali* platters of Gujarat to the *pani puri* of Mumbai. Something all Indian dishes have in common is a remarkable harmony of spice, from the subtle honeyed hue of saffron in *kulfi* to the robust earthiness of cumin and fenugreek in a dal. You may be inclined to think that recipes with ingredients lists calling for so many spices will be difficult, but stocking up on ground coriander, garam masala and anise-like fennel seeds is not that much of an effort, and when you try these dishes you'll be glad you went to the trouble. As you cook your way through this chapter, you'll learn that cumin and mustard seeds need to be tempered first, in sizzling hot oil to release their beautiful aromas. And that stirring garam masala into a dish toward the end of cooking leaves the more delicate flavors of cardamom and cloves intact.

Dining etiquette in India is quite unlike that in the Western world. Food is very often eaten with the right hand, as touch is believed to be an important element of the eating experience. Lunch or dinner is generally served on large, round metallic platters, with small dollops of curries, chutneys and vegetables to accompany your roti or rice.

I still remember the feasts my grandmother would whip up for Diwali, the kitchen counters buried under plates of fried bread and delectable curries. When nostalgia hits me, I always cook Indian food. To me, Indian food means comfort. It means family. And home.

How to make samosas

Cut the square wrapper into three pieces.

Fold the bottom corner of one strip up to meet the midpoint of the opposite edge.

Apply the flour paste along the edges that are crossed out in the diagram.

Fold the flap upwards, so that the 2 edges marked * lie on top of each other. Make sure the corner circled is tight and has no holes.

Filling

Fill the "cone" pocket you have created with a tablespoon of filling.

Spread the flour paste along the crossed out edges with your finger.

Fold the filled pocket up along the circled edges, keeping it tight. Press it down to seal the samosa along the edges with flour paste.

Cauliflower samosas

Makes 30 small samosas
—

Prep time: 30 minutes
Cooking time: 40 minutes

Filling
1 teaspoon vegetable oil
½ teaspoon mustard seeds
½ teaspoon cumin seeds
¼ teaspoon fennel seeds
1 white onion, finely chopped
2 garlic cloves, finely chopped
1 cm ginger, finely chopped
2 cups (250 g) very finely
  chopped cauliflower
1 tablespoon plus 1 teaspoon
  curry powder
½ cup (40 g) TVP granules,
  prepared (page 25)
½ cup (75 g) frozen peas
½–¾ teaspoon salt

¼ cup plus 1 tablespoon
  (50 g) all-purpose flour
10 square wheat spring roll
  wrappers, each cut into 3
  equal strips
¼ cup (60 ml) plant milk
1 tablespoon plus 1 teaspoon
  rice syrup
¼ cup (40 g) sesame or
  poppy seeds, to garnish –
  optional
Mint chutney or Mango
  chutney (page 45), to serve

This is the perfect appetizer or snack for when you have friends round – who can say no to a samosa? My version is bursting with gloriously curried cauliflower and peas and, to make things even easier, I use frozen spring roll wrappers, which you can find in the freezer aisle of most Asian supermarkets.

For the filling, place a large nonstick saucepan over medium heat, then add the oil, mustard, cumin and fennel seeds and fry until fragrant and the mustard seeds start to "pop." Add the onion, garlic and ginger and fry for 3–5 minutes, until the onions are translucent and you can smell the sizzling garlic. Add the cauliflower, curry powder and the drained TVP and fry for a further 5 minutes. Now add the peas and ¼ cup (60 ml) water, cover with a lid and bring to a boil. Reduce the heat and cook until the filling is dry and you can see no more water in the pan, 5–8 minutes. Take off the heat, stir in the salt and then taste, and adjust the seasoning if necessary.

When you're ready to assemble the samosas, preheat the oven to 350°F (180°C) and grease a large baking sheet.

Mix the flour with 3 tablespoons water to make a smooth paste. Fold and fill the samosas as shown opposite, then lay them on the baking sheet. Mix the milk and syrup together to make a glaze. Brush the tops of the samosas with the glaze and sprinkle with a few sesame or poppy seeds, if you like.

Bake for 15–20 minutes, until the samosas are golden and crisp, then serve with chutney.

Fennel and parsnip tarka dal

Serves 4

—

Prep time: 20 minutes
Cooking time: 40 minutes

1 cup (200 g) red split lentils
1 teaspoon ground turmeric
2 bay leaves
4 cups (1 liter) vegetable
    stock
2 fennel bulbs, tops and roots
    cut off, outer layer peeled
    with a vegetable peeler,
    then diced
1 large parsnip, peeled and
    cut into 2-inch (5 cm) long
    batons
1 teaspoon vegetable oil
1 teaspoon cumin seeds
¾ teaspoon salt
1 bunch (75 g) cilantro, leaves
    only, finely chopped
¼ cup (25 g) sliced almonds,
    toasted
Naan breads (page 36), rice
    or chapatis, to serve

Tempering
1 teaspoon vegetable oil
1 tablespoon plus 1 teaspoon
    mustard seeds
1 teaspoon fenugreek seeds
1 tablespoon plus 1 teaspoon
    cumin seeds pinch of
    asafetida – optional
1 red onion, finely chopped
2 inches (5 cm) ginger, finely
    chopped
2 green chilies, seeded and
    finely chopped
2 large tomatoes, diced
1 teaspoon chili powder

If I had to eat one meal for the rest of my life, I would choose dal in a heartbeat. It was a weekly staple when I was growing up, and I used to tear into fresh rounds of homemade chapati just to mop my plate clean. This is a version I first made when I was homesick and in desperate need of a winter treat. Parsnip and fennel are perhaps unusual additions to a dal, but together they give it an almost herby, anise-like twang.

Preheat the oven to 400°F (200°C).

Put the lentils, turmeric, bay leaves and stock in a large saucepan over medium heat. Bring to a boil, then reduce to a simmer, cover and leave to cook gently for about 30 minutes.

In a bowl, mix the fennel and parsnip with the oil, cumin and ¼ teaspoon of the salt. Transfer onto a baking sheet and roast for 25–30 minutes, until tender.

Meanwhile, in a medium nonstick frying pan, temper the spices: Pour in the oil and set over medium heat. When it's hot, fry the mustard, fenugreek, cumin seeds and asafetida, if using, until they're fragrant, the mustard seeds "pop" and the pungent aroma of the asafetida starts to subside. Add the onion, ginger and chilies, and continue to fry until the onion is soft and translucent. Pour in the tomatoes and chili powder, and cook for a further 3–4 minutes, until the tomatoes have softened.

When the lentils are creamy and ready, season with the remaining ½ teaspoon of salt. Pour in the tempered spices and oil, then add the roasted fennel and parsnip, and mix well.

Garnish with the cilantro leaves and sliced almonds, and serve with naan breads, rice or chapatis.

Creamy spinach curry with crispy tofu

Serves 4

—

Prep time: 20 minutes
Cooking time: 30 minutes

1 block (400 g) extra-firm
tofu, pressed (page 25) and
cut into cubes
1 teaspoon ground cumin
1 tablespoon plus 1 teaspoon
nutritional yeast
1 tablespoon plus 1 teaspoon
vegetable oil
vegan yogurt, shredded
ginger and lime wedges, to
garnish

Spinach curry
4 cups (250 g) firmly packed
spinach leaves, or 1½ cups
(200 g) thawed frozen
spinach
½ cup (125 ml) vegetable
stock
1 cup (250 ml) plant milk
1 small white onion, diced
4 garlic cloves, finely chopped
1 inch (2.5 cm) ginger, finely
chopped
1 red chili, seeded and sliced
1 large tomato, diced
½ teaspoon salt
1–2 teaspoons white sugar
1 teaspoon garam masala
2½ tablespoons nutritional
yeast

This is a plant-based version of *palak paneer.* Tofu is a wonderful substitute for mild and milky paneer cheese – you won't miss the cheese! If you are using frozen spinach for this, thaw it in the microwave for 3–5 minutes or let it defrost at room temperature, then place in a sieve and use your hands to squeeze out as much of the water as you can before measuring.

Toss the tofu cubes in a bowl with the cumin, nutritional yeast and a good pinch of salt. Put the oil in a medium nonstick frying pan over medium-high heat and fry the tofu until crisp and golden on all sides, 5–7 minutes (2–3 minutes on each side).

Put all the spinach curry ingredients in a blender and blend until smooth. Pour into a large saucepan over medium heat and bring to a boil. Add the tofu, turn the heat down to low and simmer until the curry has thickened, about 15 minutes.

Serve warm, garnished with a drizzle of vegan yogurt, shredded ginger and lime wedges.

Tandoori cauliflower "wings"

 GF *Use rice flour instead of wheat flour.*

Serves 4

—

Prep time: 20 minutes (plus marinating time)
Cooking time: 50 minutes

Batter
½ cup (130 g) vegan yogurt
1 cup (250 ml) plant milk
¾ cup (100 g) all-purpose flour, sifted
1 cm ginger, finely chopped
2 garlic cloves, finely chopped
½ teaspoon chili powder
1 teaspoon garam masala
¼ teaspoon salt

1 head of cauliflower, cut into florets – about 4 cups (500 g)

Glaze
1 cup (250 ml) tomato passata
2½ tablespoons rice syrup
½ teaspoon ground cumin
¼ teaspoon ground turmeric
1 teaspoon garam masala
¼ teaspoon salt

mint leaves, to garnish
Mint and cucumber raita (page 41), to serve

These tandoori "wings" are simultaneously silky and explosive, and tantalizingly moreish. If you aren't the biggest fan of cauliflower, hear me out: The marinade, not the cauliflower, is the star here, so it is sure to satisfy cauliflower lover and hater alike.

Combine all the ingredients for the batter in a bowl, then pour it into a large ziplock bag and add the cauliflower florets. Seal the bag and shake it to cover each floret with batter, then leave in the fridge to marinate for at least 20 minutes, or overnight.

When you're ready to cook the "wings," preheat the oven to 450°F (230°C) and line a baking sheet with parchment paper. Place the cauliflower florets on the sheet, making sure each one is well coated in the batter, and bake for 25 minutes.

Meanwhile, mix all the glaze ingredients together in a shallow bowl.

Take the cauliflower florets out of the oven and, one by one, dip them into the glaze, shaking off any excess and then placing them back on the baking sheet. When all the cauliflower florets are glazed, return them to the oven and bake for another 20–25 minutes, until the glaze looks dry and the florets are ever so slightly caramelized.

Pile the "wings" onto a platter and scatter with mint leaves. Serve with a bowl of raita, for dipping.

Naan breads: plain, garlic and Peshwari

Makes 8
—
Prep time: 35 minutes (plus proofing time)
Cooking time: 15 minutes

½ cup (125 ml) lukewarm
    plant milk
1 teaspoon white sugar
1 packet (2½ teaspoons)
    active dry yeast
¼ cup (70 g) vegan yogurt
¼ cup (60 ml) aquafaba
    (page 11)
2½ tablespoons vegetable
    oil, plus extra for greasing
2½ cups (375 g) all-purpose
    flour, plus extra for dusting
½ teaspoon salt

For garlic naan
5 garlic cloves, finely chopped
¼ cup (60 g) vegan butter,
    melted
¼ cup (15 g) finely chopped
    cilantro

For Peshwari naan
½ cup (85 g) raisins
½ cup (50 g) sliced almonds
½ cup (45 g) desiccated
    coconut

Naan breads are traditionally baked in a clay oven, giving them their distinctive burnished exterior and fluffy interior. To get a similar result at home, I use a combination of baking in the oven and charring over an open flame.

In a large bowl or the bowl of an electric mixer, stir together the milk, sugar and yeast. Leave for 5 minutes, or until frothy, then stir in the yogurt, aquafaba and oil. Sift in the flour and salt and mix well. Now knead the dough, either using the mixer's dough hook or by hand on a well-floured countertop, until smooth and elastic – this should take 7–10 minutes. Shape it into a ball and put it back in the bowl, then cover with a clean kitchen towel. Leave somewhere warm to rise until doubled in size, about an hour.

Preheat the oven to 350°F (180°C) and oil two large baking sheets. Punch the risen dough down, to knock out some of the air, then transfer onto a floured countertop and divide into eight. Roll into balls, then flatten and stretch into ovals about 3 mm thick. Place on the baking sheets, cover again and leave to rise for 10 minutes. (If you don't have enough baking sheets – or oven space – to accommodate all the breads at once, you can cook them in batches.)

Bake the breads for 7–8 minutes, until firm but not browned. If you have a gas stove, use tongs to hold each bread over a low flame until golden all over and lightly charred in places. If you have any other type of stove, or if you prefer not to cook directly over a flame, place a nonstick frying pan or grill pan over low heat and sear each bread on both sides.

For garlic naan, knead half the garlic into the dough, making sure it is evenly distributed, then proof and cook as above. Brush the cooked naan breads with vegan butter and sprinkle with the rest of the garlic and the cilantro.

For Peshwari naan, mix the raisins, almonds and coconut together. Roughly flatten each dough ball, place a heaped tablespoon of raisin mixture in the middle and bring up the sides to seal it in the center of the ball. Shape, proof and bake as above.

Dosas

Serves 4
—

Prep time: 20 minutes
Cooking time: 30 minutes

1 cup (185 g) cooked medium-
   or long-grain rice
1 cup (160 g) rice flour
½ cup (45 g) oat flour*
1 teaspoon fenugreek seeds
¼ cup (70 g) vegan yogurt
½ teaspoon salt
¼ teaspoon baking soda
2½ tablespoons lemon juice
vegetable oil, for frying
Coconut chutney (page 40),
   Dal makhani (page 42) or
   Fennel and parsnip tarka
   dal (page 31), to serve

Every country has its pancakes. And in South India the dosa reigns supreme. It is traditionally made with fermented rice and lentil batter, which is spread whisper-thin on a *tawa* (a large Indian frying pan) and fried until golden, then served rolled up like a scroll. They are crispy, tangy and irresistible when doused in coconut chutney. While fermented foods are great for you, fermenting dosa batter requires preplanning and waiting. My version is a quicker alternative that uses cooked rice – perfect for using up any leftovers from the night before.

Put the rice, rice flour, oat flour, fenugreek and 1½ cups (375 ml) water in a blender and mix until smooth: You should not be able to feel any grit when you rub a little of the batter between your fingers. Add the yogurt, salt, baking soda and lemon juice and blend again so everything is thoroughly mixed.

Place a large nonstick frying pan (or a well-seasoned *tawa*) over medium-high heat and oil it lightly, using a paper towel to wipe out any excess. To check if the pan is ready, flick a little water onto it: If it sizzles, you can start making your dosas.

Pour ¼ cup (60 ml) batter into the center of your pan, then use the back of a ladle or large spoon to spread it out in a circular motion, forming a thin round pancake. Let the dosa cook for 30–40 seconds. When it is starting to firm up, drizzle a small amount of oil over the top and let it cook for another 60 seconds or until it is golden and crisp underneath. Use a spatula to loosen the sides and fold it over – you do not have to cook the other side. Remove from the pan and continue with the remaining batter.

Serve the dosas hot, with coconut chutney and dal.

* To make oat flour, place rolled oats in a blender and grind until fine – measure out the required amount after grinding.

Coconut chutney

Prep time: 10 minutes
Cooking time: 3 minutes

½ cup (45 g) desiccated
  coconut
1 large green chili, seeded
½ small white onion, chopped
1 inch (2.5 cm) ginger
1 tablespoon Roasted
  chickpeas (page 22) –
  optional
1 teaspoon coconut oil
1 tablespoon black mustard
  seeds
½ teaspoon cumin seeds
7 curry leaves – optional
¼ teaspoon salt

Of all the Indian chutneys, coconut chutney is by far my favorite. It's silky and delightfully creamy. Freckled with mustard seeds, it is the perfect partner to a dosa or roti, or alongside any curry. If you can find fresh coconut, use that instead of the desiccated kind: You'll need ½ cup (40 g) freshly grated coconut. Because it will be moister, it's a good idea to reduce the amount of water you use by about a tablespoon.

Put the coconut, chili, onion, ginger, ¼ cup (60 ml) water and the roasted chickpeas, if using, in a food processor. Blend to a smooth paste, then pour into a glass serving bowl and set aside.

Heat the oil in a small frying pan over medium heat and fry the mustard and cumin seeds until fragrant and the mustard seeds start to "pop." Add the curry leaves, if using, and cook until crisp. Pour the spice-tempered oil over the coconut mixture and stir it in. Add the salt, then taste and adjust the seasoning if necessary.

This will keep for 4–5 days in the fridge when made with desiccated coconut (if you've used fresh coconut, it will only last 2–3 days).

NOTE You can also make this chutney chunky, as I prefer. Instead of processing everything together at the start, just chop the onion, ginger and chili very finely, then mix with the coconut and water – leave out the roasted chickpeas in this version.

Mint and cucumber raita

Serves 4
—

Prep time: 10 minutes
**Cooking time: no cooking
needed**

1 cup (260 g) vegan yogurt
1 cm ginger, finely chopped
¼ cup (15 g) chopped mint
  leaves
juice of ½ lemon
¼ teaspoon garam masala
¼ cup (45 g) grated
  cucumber, squeezed to
  remove excess water
  before measuring
pinch of salt

A raita is just what is needed when you are tucking into a spicy curry: It offers a cool, zesty contrast. I always whip up a raita as a side dish when cooking Indian food, because it goes with pretty much anything! Try it with Tandoori cauliflower "wings" (page 35) or Sweet potato and onion pakoras (page 46). Easy, peasy, lemon squeezy. Quite literally.

Combine all the ingredients in a bowl and keep in the fridge. Raita is best served chilled.

Dal makhani

Serves 4
—
Prep time: 20 minutes (plus soaking time)
Cooking time: 45 minutes

1 cup (220 g) whole urad dal (black gram), soaked for 4 hours or overnight*
one 15-ounce (425 g) can kidney beans, rinsed and drained
1 teaspoon vegetable oil
1 teaspoon cumin seeds
pinch of asafetida – optional
1 large white onion, finely chopped
6 garlic cloves, finely chopped
1 inch (2.5 cm) ginger, finely chopped
2 tomatoes, diced
½–1 teaspoon chili powder
½ cup (125 ml) plant milk
1 teaspoon salt
1 teaspoon garam masala
¼ cup (60 ml) vegan yogurt
cilantro leaves and chopped cashews, to garnish
Tomato kasundi (page 44), to serve

Dal makhani is an investment. It takes time to soak the lentils and then to coax them into a creamy and dreamy dal over a gentle heat. But it is an investment you will not regret. While this is usually made with an abundance of butter and cream, mine is a lighter version but just as luscious. You will be mopping your plate with tufts of naan bread, and that's a promise.

In a large saucepan, bring the urad dal, kidney beans and 4 cups (1 liter) water to a boil. Reduce to a simmer and cook for 30 minutes, or until the urad dal is cooked through and no longer crunchy.

Meanwhile, heat the vegetable oil in a medium nonstick frying pan and fry the cumin seeds and asafetida over medium heat until they're aromatic and the smell of the asafetida starts to mellow out, about 1 minute. Add the onion, garlic and ginger, and fry until the onions are soft and translucent. Next, add the tomatoes and chili powder and cook over low heat until the tomatoes are saucy, about 3–5 minutes.

When the urad dal is cooked, use a potato masher to mash the urad dal and kidney beans into their cooking water. This causes the beans to release their starch and allows the dal to thicken further.

Return the pan to the heat and stir in the onion mixture, along with the milk and salt. Continue to cook until the dal is thick and creamy, about 15 minutes, then stir in the garam masala. Take it off the heat and drizzle with the vegan yogurt. Garnish with the cilantro leaves and chopped cashews, then serve with tomato kasundi.

* Urad dal can be tricky to find if you don't have an Asian grocer nearby, but green mung beans will also work here.

Tomato kasundi

Prep time: 15 minutes
Cooking time: 1½ hours

1 tablespoon plus 1 teaspoon
   vegetable oil
1 tablespoon plus 1 teaspoon
   black mustard seeds
1 tablespoon plus 1 teaspoon
   ground turmeric
2½ tablespoons ground
   cumin
2½ tablespoons chili powder
2 inches (5 cm) ginger, finely
   chopped
4 garlic cloves, finely chopped
1 green chili, seeded and
   chopped
⅔ cup (170 ml) apple cider
   vinegar
two 14.5-ounce (411 g) cans
   diced tomatoes
⅓ cup (60 g) lightly packed
   light brown sugar
1 teaspoon salt

This fiery chutney is a great thing to whip up and it stores beautifully in the fridge. Think of it as a relish akin to ketchup – tangy and saucy, but with a pretty good kick to it. You can, of course, cut back on the chili powder if spice is not your thing.

Pour the oil into a nonstick saucepan over medium heat and fry the mustard seeds, turmeric, cumin and chili powder for 5 minutes. Add the ginger, garlic, green chili and 2½ tablespoons of the vinegar and cook for another 5 minutes.

Finally, add the tomatoes, sugar, salt and the rest of the vinegar and simmer for about 1 hour over very low heat. The chutney is ready when you can see some oil separating from the tomatoes and sitting on the surface.

Allow to cool completely, then store in a sterilized glass jar in the fridge for up to 2 weeks.

Mint chutney

Serves 6–8

—

Prep time: 10 minutes
Cooking time: 5 minutes

1 teaspoon vegetable oil
1 teaspoon mustard seeds
1 cup lightly packed (20 g)
  mint leaves
½ cup (45 g) desiccated
  coconut
2 green chilies, seeded
1 teaspoon tamarind paste
¼ teaspoon salt
¼ cup (60 ml) coconut milk,
  plus extra for blending if
  necessary
1 tablespoon plus 1 teaspoon
  Roasted chickpeas (page
  22) – optional

This fantastically fresh and zingy chutney packs a punch. It adds bold flavor alongside any Indian finger food, such as Sweet potato and onion pakoras (page 46) or Cauliflower samosas (page 29).

Heat the oil in a frying pan over high heat and fry the mustard seeds until they start to "pop." Add the mint leaves and continue to fry until wilted.

Transfer the mixture to a food processor, then add the desiccated coconut, chilies, tamarind, salt, coconut milk and chickpeas, if using. Blend to a smooth puree, adding more coconut milk if needed, a tablespoon at a time.

This will keep, covered, for 3–4 days in the fridge, and is best served chilled.

Mango chutney

Serves 6–8

—

Prep time: 15 minutes
Cooking time: 15 minutes

2 mangoes, flesh only, cubed
1 inch (2.5 cm) ginger, finely
  chopped
¼ teaspoon ground cumin
pinch of paprika
½ cup (175 g) rice syrup
8 cardamom pods, seeds only
1 tablespoon plus 1 teaspoon
  lemon juice
pinch of salt

The ultimate condiment. While mango chutney is the perfect accompaniment to any Indian main dish, it is equally delicious slathered onto sandwiches and wraps. This is a quick version, perfect for using up any mangoes that are threatening to become overripe.

In a food processor or blender, puree a third of the mango with the ginger, cumin, paprika and syrup and ¼ cup (60 ml) water until smooth. Pour the puree into a saucepan, along with the rest of the mango, cardamom seeds, lemon juice and salt. Bring to a boil and then let it simmer until thickened, about 10 minutes – when it's ready, the mango should be soft and tender.

Transfer to a sterilized glass jar and store in the refrigerator for up to 4 weeks. The chutney is best eaten chilled.

Sweet potato and onion pakoras

GF

**Makes 12 (enough for
4 as a side)**

—

**Prep time: 15 minutes
Cooking time: 20 minutes**

¾ cup (90 g) chickpea flour
¼ cup (45 g) rice flour
1½ teaspoons cornstarch
2 teaspoons garam masala
½ teaspoon ground turmeric
1 teaspoon ground cumin
¼ teaspoon chili powder
1 cm ginger, finely chopped
½ teaspoon salt
¼ teaspoon black pepper
½ cup (125 ml) plant milk
1 white onion, peeled and
    spiralized
1 sweet potato, peeled and
    spiralized
oil, for brushing
mint leaves, Mint or Mango
    chutney (page 45), to serve

These pakoras are melt-in-your-mouth gorgeous and very versatile. You can substitute any of the vegetables here for whatever you have on hand, such as spiralized zucchini or shredded cabbage. Serving these golden fritters with a mint chutney, or some Mint and cucumber raita (page 41), injects a hint of freshness. If you do not have a spiralizer, just use a julienne peeler to shred the vegetables, or cut them into thin strips.

Preheat the oven to 450°F (230°C), and line a large baking sheet with parchment paper.

Sift the flours and cornstarch into a large bowl and add the spices, ginger, salt and pepper. Gradually add the milk, whisking as you go, until no lumps remain. Fold in the onion and sweet potato.

Use a large spoon to drop dollops of batter onto the prepared baking sheet, trimming off any strands with scissors, if necessary. Bake the pakoras for 15 minutes, then lightly brush the tops with oil and return to the oven for another 5 minutes, or until they are golden and firm.

Let the pakoras cool slightly before serving with mint leaves and chutney.

Vegan "butter chicken"

Use 1 pound (450 g) extra-firm tofu, or two 15-ounce (425 g) cans chickpeas in place of seitan.

Serves 4
—

Prep time: 20 minutes (plus soaking time)
Cooking time: 25 minutes

1 teaspoon vegetable oil
1 teaspoon cumin seeds
½ teaspoon coriander seeds
1 white onion, diced
4 garlic cloves, finely chopped
1 cm ginger, finely chopped
½ teaspoon ground turmeric
¼ teaspoon chili powder
pinch of ground cinnamon
2 cups (500 ml) tomato passata
¼ cup (40 g) cashews, soaked for 1 hour
½ cup (125 ml) plant milk
1 teaspoon white sugar
1 teaspoon lemon juice
pinch of black pepper
½ teaspoon salt
2 teaspoons garam masala
1 recipe Seitan "chicken" (page 22), torn into small strips
cilantro leaves, to garnish
lime wedges, rice and Naan breads (page 36), to serve

My butter chicken has neither butter nor chicken, so perhaps calling it that is somewhat misleading. But I promise it's robust and feisty enough to sway the most committed carnivore. . . .

Heat the oil in a large nonstick saucepan over medium heat and fry the cumin and coriander seeds until fragrant, about 1 minute. Next, add the onion, garlic and ginger and fry until the onion is soft and translucent, adding a small splash of water if it begins to stick. Stir in the turmeric, chili powder and cinnamon, then pour in the passata. Drain the cashews and add them to the pan as well, then bring to a gentle simmer and cook for 5 minutes.

Transfer the mixture to a large blender, add the milk, sugar, lemon juice, pepper and salt, and puree to make a smooth sauce. Carefully pour the sauce back into the saucepan (it will still be very hot), then put the pan back over medium heat and add the garam masala and torn pieces of seitan chicken. Simmer gently for 5–10 minutes, to let it reduce a little and to heat up the seitan.

Garnish the "butter chicken" with cilantro leaves, then serve with lime wedges, rice and naan breads.

Chana masala fries

Serves 4

—

Prep time: 20 minutes
Cooking time: 30 minutes

4 potatoes, about 21 ounces
    (600 g) in total
1 tablespoon plus 1 teaspoon
    garam masala
1 tablespoon plus 1 teaspoon
    coconut oil
juice of ½ lime
½ teaspoon salt

Chana masala
1 teaspoon vegetable oil
2 teaspoons cumin seeds
pinch of asafetida – optional
1 white onion, diced
3 garlic cloves, finely chopped
1 inch (2.5 cm) ginger, finely
    chopped
½ teaspoon ground turmeric
4 tomatoes, chopped
two 15-ounce (425 g) cans
    chickpeas, drained
1 teaspoon garam masala
1 tablespoon chana masala
    spice blend* (or garam
    masala)
1 teaspoon white sugar
½ teaspoon salt
¾ teaspoon mango powder
    (*amchoor*) or 2 teaspoons
    lemon juice
juice of ½ lemon
chopped cilantro and pickled
    red onion, to garnish

The secret to getting a restaurant-like result lies in the *chana masala* spice blend, which can be found online or in Asian supermarkets. However, if you can't get it, simply use more garam masala. Do also keep an eye out for mango powder (*amchoor*), as it imparts a distinctive tartness, making all the difference to the taste.

Preheat the oven to 400°F (200°C), and line a large baking sheet with parchment paper. Cut the potatoes into thin wedges and let them soak in a bowl of cold water for 10 minutes, then pat dry with paper towel. Place the wedges on the baking sheet and sprinkle with the garam masala, oil, lime juice and salt. Toss well to coat, then bake for 30 minutes, flipping the wedges halfway.

Meanwhile, for the chana masala, pour the oil into a large saucepan over medium-high heat and fry the cumin seeds and asafetida, if using, until the cumin is aromatic and the asafetida has lost its pungency. Add the onion, garlic, ginger and turmeric. Continue to fry until the onion is soft and translucent and you can smell the sizzling garlic. Add the tomatoes, bring to a simmer and cook until the tomatoes are softened and saucy, about 5 minutes. Add the chickpeas, garam masala and chana masala spice blend and stir well. Cook for another 5 minutes to thicken it slightly – it's ready when it is more gravy-like and no longer watery. Stir in the sugar, salt, mango powder and lemon juice. Serve the chana masala on top of the spiced potato wedges, garnished with cilantro and pickled red onion.

* This has chili powder in it, so add less of it if you don't like spicy food, using more garam masala instead.

Butter bean tikka curry

Serves 4
—

Prep time: 20 minutes
Cooking time: 25 minutes

¼ cup (70 g) vegan yogurt
3 garlic cloves, finely chopped
1 inch (2.5 cm) ginger, finely
    chopped
½ teaspoon ground turmeric
1 teaspoon garam masala
¼ teaspoon chili powder
½ teaspoon salt
two 15-ounce (425 g) cans
    butter beans, drained

Tikka curry
1 teaspoon vegetable oil
1 large white onion, chopped
2 garlic cloves, finely chopped
2 inches (5 cm) ginger, finely
    chopped
1 bay leaf
1 teaspoon ground cumin
1 teaspoon ground coriander
½ teaspoon ground cinnamon
1 tablespoon plus 1 teaspoon
    garam masala
2 teaspoons smoked paprika
2 tablespoons tomato paste
3 large tomatoes, chopped,
    or 1 cup (250 ml) tomato
    passata
¼ cup (25 g) chopped
    cilantro stems
¼ cup (70 g) vegan yogurt
1 tablespoon plus 1 teaspoon
    rice syrup
1 teaspoon lemon juice
Naan breads (page 36) or
    rice, to serve

Butter beans are one of my favorite beans. They are hearty and – for want of a better word – buttery. Their starchiness works well in this tikka curry, but if you prefer a different bean, feel free to substitute.

Preheat the oven to 400°F (200°C) and grease a baking sheet. In a large bowl, mix together the yogurt, garlic, ginger, turmeric, garam masala, chili powder and salt. Add the butter beans and stir to coat well, then transfer onto a baking sheet and bake for 15–17 minutes, until the beans start to look dry and a bit crisper.

Meanwhile, for the tikka curry, heat the oil in a large nonstick saucepan over medium heat. Fry the onion, garlic and ginger for about 2 minutes, until fragrant and the onions have softened. Add the bay leaf and spices and fry for another minute until aromatic. Next, add the tomato paste, chopped tomatoes and cilantro stems, then cover and bring to a boil. Lower the heat and let it simmer, covered, for 5 minutes. Add the beans when they're ready, along with the yogurt, syrup and lemon juice. Bring back to a boil, then remove from the heat.

Serve warm, with naan breads or rice.

Kofta curry

 GF *Use gluten-free bread crumbs.*

Serves 5–6

—

Prep time: 20 minutes
Cooking time: 40 minutes

Koftas
½ cup (110 g) short-grain rice
½ cup (100 g) red split lentils
1 teaspoon vegetable oil
1 white onion, chopped
2 cups (200 g) very finely
    chopped mushrooms
1 Flax egg (page 21)
1 cup (140 g) bread crumbs
2½ tablespoons garam
    masala
½ teaspoon salt
¼ teaspoon black pepper

Sauce
1 tablespoon ground coriander
2 teaspoons ground cumin
½ teaspoon ground turmeric
½–1 teaspoon chili powder
1 teaspoon garam masala
2 cups (500 ml) tomato
    passata
1½ cups (375 ml) vegetable
    stock
½ cup (125 ml) plant milk
1 teaspoon white sugar
1 tablespoon plus 1 teaspoon
    lemon juice
1 bay leaf
½ cup (130 g) vegan yogurt
    or ½ cup (125 ml) coconut
    milk

chopped cilantro, to garnish

Lentils add a little extra protein to make this spin on the usual potato-based kofta curry a meal that is both filling and nourishing.

Preheat the oven to 400°F (200°C) and line a large baking sheet with parchment paper.

For the koftas, put the rice and 3 cups (750 ml) water in a large saucepan, then bring to a boil and cook for 5 minutes. Add the lentils and cook for another 10–15 minutes, until both rice and lentils are tender.

Meanwhile, heat the oil in a large nonstick frying pan and fry the onion. Add the mushrooms and continue to fry until the mushrooms are wilted and soft.

When the rice and lentils are ready, drain and mash with a potato masher. Add the fried onions and mushrooms, leaving behind in the pan any liquid the mushrooms may have released. Stir in the Flax egg, bread crumbs, garam masala, salt and pepper, then shape the kofta mixture into about twenty balls. Place on the baking sheet and bake for 15–20 minutes, until firm and slightly golden.

While the koftas are cooking, put all the sauce ingredients except the yogurt in a large saucepan. Bring to a boil, then reduce to a simmer and cook for about 15–20 minutes to thicken. Stir in the yogurt and, when they are ready, add the koftas. Serve hot, garnished with cilantro.

NOTE If using leftover rice, use 1 cup (185 g) cooked rice. Cook the lentils separately in 1 cup (250 ml) boiling water before draining, then mash the rice and lentils together.

Kedgeree

 GF

Make sure the smoked tofu you are using does not contain soy sauce.

Serves 4
—

Prep time: 20 minutes
Cooking time: 25 minutes

20 cherry tomatoes, halved
1 teaspoon vegetable oil
1 white onion, diced
2 cardamom pods, crushed
½ teaspoon ground turmeric
1 bay leaf
1 tablespoon plus 1 teaspoon
   curry powder
½ teaspoon ground coriander
1½ cups (300 g) basmati rice
2¼ cups (560 ml) vegetable
   stock
½ teaspoon salt
1 cup (140 g) frozen peas
¼ teaspoon black pepper
1 tablespoon plus 1 teaspoon
   lemon juice
one 8-ounce (227 g) block
   smoked tofu, cubed
soy yogurt, lemon wedges
   and chopped cilantro, to
   serve

This is a Western dish that takes its inspiration from Indian *khichari*, a rice and lentil dish. That's why it calls for curry powder, something you wouldn't usually see in a traditional Indian recipe, where individual spices are usually blended together instead. Still, its South Asian roots mean that kedgeree is wonderfully perfumed, and my version here is tossed with blistered tomatoes. It's a joy to eat hot or cold, for breakfast or for lunch – you decide.

Place the cherry tomatoes under a hot broiler and cook for 10 minutes, until plump and blistered.

Meanwhile, put the oil in a large nonstick saucepan over medium heat and fry the onion until soft and translucent, about 4 minutes. Add the cardamom, turmeric, bay leaf, curry powder and ground coriander. Stir to coat the onions well in the spices, then add the rice, again stirring well to coat. Pour in the stock and bring to a boil. Add the salt and peas, then cover the pan, reduce the heat to low and leave to simmer until the rice is cooked and no longer crunchy, about 10–12 minutes.

When the rice is done, stir in the black pepper, lemon juice, smoked tofu and cherry tomatoes.

Serve the kedgeree warm, with a dollop of soy yogurt, a wedge of lemon and some cilantro.

Serves 2
—
Prep time: 5 minutes
Cooking time: no cooking needed

1 cup (250 ml) chilled plant milk
1 cup (260 g) vegan yogurt
½ teaspoon black salt (or regular salt)
½ teaspoon roasted ground cumin

Serves 2
—
Prep time: 10 minutes
Cooking time: no cooking needed

2 ripe mangoes, flesh only, cubed, or 1 cup (250 ml) mango puree
1 cup (250 ml) chilled plant milk
¼ teaspoon ground cardamom, or the seeds from 4 cardamom pods
½ cup (130 g) vegan yogurt
2–3 ice cubes – optional
1–2 tablespoons white sugar

Salted cumin lassi

This is the classic salted lassi, spiced with cumin. To roast ground cumin, briefly toss it in a dry frying pan over medium-low heat until fragrant.

Put all the ingredients in a blender and blend until smooth.

Sweet mango and cardamom lassi

Traditionally, lassi is a savory drink, but I like mine sweet and fruity, laced with the delicate perfume of cardamom. If you're trying to avoid refined sugars, feel free to use raw sugar or brown rice syrup to sweeten your lassi. With lassi, there is endless room for creativity. I've included several spins on the sweet version below, just to get you started.

Put all the ingredients except the sugar in a blender and blend until smooth. Taste, and add sugar if necessary – the amount you'll need depends on the sweetness of the mangoes and how sweet you like your lassi.

For Banana lassi, replace the mango with 2 bananas.

For Strawberry and rose lassi, replace the mango and cardamom with 1 cup (160 g) diced strawberries and ¼ teaspoon rose water.

For Ginger pineapple lassi, replace the mango and cardamom with 1 cup (160 g) pineapple chunks and 1–2 teaspoons grated ginger.

For Orange and cinnamon lassi, replace the mango and cardamom with 2 peeled and chopped oranges and ¼ teaspoon ground cinnamon.

For Papaya and lime lassi, replace the mango and cardamom with 1½ cups (240 g) papaya cubes and the juice of 1 lime.

Creamy carrot halwa

 GF

Serves 4
—

Prep time: 15 minutes
Cooking time: 30 minutes

2½ cups firmly packed
    (390 g) grated carrot
2½ cups (625 ml) plant milk
¼ teaspoon ground
    cardamom, or the seeds
    from 4 cardamom pods
½ teaspoon ground turmeric
    – optional
1–2 tablespoons rice syrup
1 tablespoon plus 1 teaspoon
    coconut oil or vegan butter
pinch of salt
¼ cup (45 g) raisins
¼ cup (40 g) pistachios (or
    cashews), chopped*
sliced almonds and
    pistachios, to garnish

At first, using grated carrot in a pudding like this might seem strange, but it is no stranger than a classic carrot cake. Here, grated carrots are stewed in a cocktail of sugar and spice, to yield a velvety dessert stippled with jewel-like raisins and emerald pistachios.

Put the grated carrot and plant milk in a medium saucepan, bring to a simmer and cook for 15 minutes. Now add the cardamom – and the turmeric, if using. Continue to cook, stirring constantly, until almost all the liquid has been absorbed. Stir in the syrup, oil and salt and cook for another 3–5 minutes, until it is still wet but there are no pools of liquid remaining around the carrots.

Finally, stir in the raisins and nuts and take it off the heat. You can eat this pudding hot, but it is equally delicious chilled. Either way, do serve it sprinkled with a few sliced almonds and some more pistachios.

* For a more affordable alternative, use pumpkin seeds.

Kulfi

Makes 4
—

Prep time: 30 minutes (plus freezing time)
Cooking time: 20 minutes

1 cup (250 ml) coconut milk
½ cup (110 g) white sugar
½ cup (125 ml) plant milk
½ cup (80 g) cashews
2 teaspoons cornstarch
¼ teaspoon ground
 cardamom, or the seeds
 from 4 cardamom pods
pinch of salt
½ teaspoon almond extract –
 optional
pinch of ground turmeric
¼ cup (35 g) chopped
 pistachios – optional
sliced almonds and roughly
 chopped pistachios, to
 garnish – optional

Indian desserts are usually infused with a hefty dose of cardamom, and *kulfi* is no exception. Cardamom is gorgeously floral and cuts through the rich, seductive coconut. I use turmeric here as saffron is quite dear, but if you do have some in your pantry, just pop two or three threads into the saucepan as you bring the coconut milk to a boil, in place of the turmeric.

Put the coconut milk and sugar in a medium saucepan over medium heat and bring to a boil. Reduce to a simmer and cook for 5 minutes.

Meanwhile, put the plant milk, cashews, cornstarch, cardamom, salt and almond extract, if using, in a blender. Blend until smooth, then pour into the pan of coconut milk. Turn the heat back up to medium and return to a boil, stirring constantly. Once the mixture has thickened, remove from the heat and leave to cool to room temperature, about 10–20 minutes. Stir in the turmeric and pistachios, if using, and then pour into four ice pop molds. Freeze for at least 4 hours, or overnight.

To serve, dip the molds in warm water for 30 seconds to loosen the kulfi, or warm the molds up between your hands. Scatter the kulfi with some sliced almonds and roughly chopped pistachios, if you like.

Cardamom fudge

**Makes 9 big or
16 small squares**

—

**Prep time: 15 minutes
Cooking time: 30 minutes**

one 13.5-ounce (400 ml) can
coconut milk
½ cup (110 g) white sugar
1 cup (120 g) chickpea flour
1 tablespoon plus 1 teaspoon
coconut oil
½ cup (65 g) chopped
cashews or pistachios, plus
extra for topping
¼ teaspoon ground cardamom
1–2 tablespoons
confectioners' sugar –
optional

Burfi is a type of Indian fudge, often eaten during Diwali. Just like its Western counterpart, *burfi* can come in many different forms. This one, called *besan burfi*, is a mélange of nuts, sugar and chickpea flour. Chickpea flour may seem like a peculiar addition to fudge, but it is quite a common component in Indian desserts, and comes with a nice hit of protein as a bonus!

Put the coconut milk and sugar in a heavy-based saucepan and place over medium-low heat. Stir well to dissolve the sugar, then simmer for 20 minutes, without stirring, until thick – you should have about 1 cup (250 ml).

Meanwhile, sift the chickpea flour straight into a large nonstick frying pan over low heat and add the coconut oil. Toast the chickpea flour until it starts to tan and begins to smell less beany and more caramelized. When it's done, pour the chickpea flour into a shallow dish, to prevent it from burning in the hot pan.

Sift the chickpea flour into a large bowl, then add the chopped nuts, cardamom and confectioners' sugar to taste, if you have a sweet tooth. When the coconut milk is ready, pass it through a sieve into the bowl and mix everything well.

Grease and line an 8-inch (20 cm) square brownie pan with parchment paper, then pour in the *burfi* mixture. Flatten it by laying a second sheet of parchment paper over the top and pressing down with a spatula. Remove the top layer of paper and, using a greased knife or pizza wheel, cut into squares. Top the *burfi* with more chopped nuts, then let it chill and set in the fridge for 1–2 hours before eating.

NOTE You can make a vanilla version of this fudge by using ½ teaspoon vanilla extract instead of the ground cardamom.

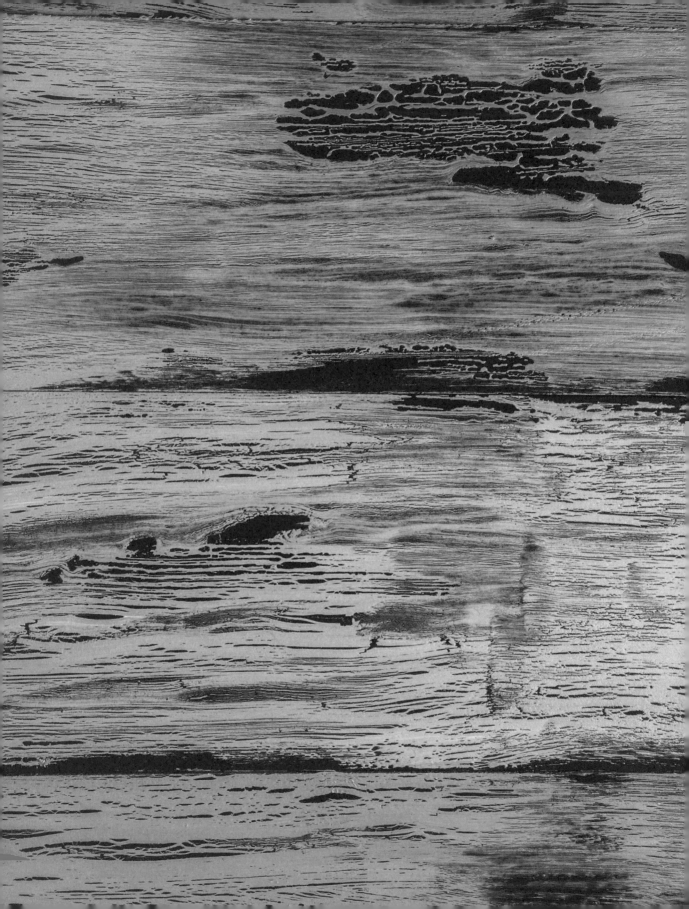

02
Thailand

Thailand is one glorious sensory overload, from the paralyzing volume of traffic in Bangkok to the bustling night markets. The streets are scattered with food stalls, home to colorful displays of perfectly ripe fruit and glistening woks of boiling-hot oil. Thai food itself is similarly enticing: It seduces and overwhelms until you just can't resist. Another?

Each dish is a delicate balancing act of salty, sweet, sour and spicy. Food here is assertive and complex. In Thailand, eating is a social event and a celebration. Friends and family gather around large tables, and dishes are almost always shared. When the food arrives, it is always dressed to impress. Adorned with intricately carved vegetables or blushing frangipani flowers, the food feeds your eyes as much as it does your belly.

Thai cooking can often be a labor of love. Massaman curries are cooked low and slow, until the coconut milk splits and reduces into a thick and velvety gravy. Curry pastes themselves are made by hand, pounded using a mortar and pestle before being fried, flinging notes of makrut lime and galangal into the air. But some dishes are quicker, only needing a fleeting kiss from a searing-hot wok. Either way, Thai cooking has a sass and personality unlike any other cuisine in the world.

Green papaya salad

Use gluten-free bread crumbs.

Serves 2 as a starter
—
Prep time: 20 minutes
Cooking time: no cooking needed

1 small green papaya

Dressing
1–2 bird's eye chilies, seeded and chopped
2 garlic cloves, crushed
1 tablespoon plus 1 teaspoon tamarind paste
1 tablespoon plus 1 teaspoon grated palm sugar
1 tablespoon plus 1 teaspoon crushed roasted peanuts
1 tablespoon plus 1 teaspoon soy sauce

10 cherry tomatoes, halved
½ cup (60 g) green beans, cut into 1-inch (2.5 cm) lengths and blanched
peanuts and lime wedges, to garnish

I was first introduced to *som tum* by my Thai friend, Minty. And after finally making my own, I can see why she adores it so much. Papaya salad is a glorious interplay of briny soy sauce, fiery chili and silky palm sugar. Although if you shy away from spice, I would suggest leaving the chilies out completely.

Should green papaya prove difficult to find at your local Asian store, try shredding some peeled and seeded cucumber, zucchini, or even sharp-tasting apples. Whatever you use, just make sure that it has firm, taut flesh, making it easy to transform into thin ribbons.

First, peel and shred the green papaya – you want to end up with about 2 cups (180 g) shredded papaya. You can do this either with a julienne peeler, on the large holes of a cheese grater, or using the grater attachment of a food processor. Stop shredding as you get close to the core containing the white, immature seeds; discard the seeds and tough core. Keep the shredded papaya in the fridge while you prepare everything else.

Next make the dressing. Using a mortar and pestle, pound the chilies and garlic to a paste. Add the tamarind, palm sugar, peanuts and soy sauce. Continue to pound until you have a smooth dressing with small flecks of peanut in it.

Toss in the cherry tomatoes and green beans and bash them just to bruise them a little. Add the shredded papaya and use the pestle to distribute it evenly and coat it with the dressing. If your mortar and pestle isn't big enough to hold everything at once, remove half of the dressing before adding the vegetables and work in two batches.

Serve the salad garnished with peanuts and lime wedges.

NOTE If you don't have a mortar and pestle, use a small blender or food processor to blitz the dressing ingredients. Pour the dressing into a bowl, add all the vegetables and use the blunt end of a rolling pin or a sturdy wooden spatula to muddle everything together and lightly bruise the vegetables.

Tofu pad thai

Use tamari instead of soy sauce.

Serves 4
—

Prep time: 20 minutes
Cooking time: 20 minutes

7 ounces (200 g) dried flat rice noodles
½ cup (60 g) chickpea flour
¼ teaspoon black salt (or regular salt)
2½ tablespoons vegetable oil
2 teaspoons tamarind paste
2½ tablespoons soy sauce
1 tablespoon plus 1 teaspoon coconut sugar (or grated palm sugar)
2 teaspoons lime juice
½–1 teaspoon sriracha
5 garlic cloves, finely chopped
3 shallots, finely diced
2 cups (300–350 g) mixed vegetables, such as grated carrot, baby corn, bean sprouts, sliced scallions
one 14-ounce (400 g) block extra-firm tofu, pressed (page 25) and cubed
⅓ cup (50 g) chopped roasted peanuts
chopped peanuts, lime wedges, bean sprouts and chopped cilantro, to garnish

Everybody loves a good pad thai. When soaking the noodles for this dish, be careful not to let them soak for too long. You want them to retain some of their crunch before you fry them. Remember, you can always add more water to the wok to soften the noodles, but you can't rescue overcooked noodles!

First, soak your noodles. Bring a saucepan of water to a boil, then take it off the heat. Add the noodles and leave to soak, completely submerged, for 4–7 minutes, until they go from translucent to white. You want them to be pliable, but not soft. Pour the noodles into a colander and rinse under cold running water until they are cool – this removes excess starch. Drain thoroughly and set aside.

Whisk together the chickpea flour, black salt and ½ cup (125 ml) water until no lumps remain. Pour a little oil into a wok or a deep nonstick frying pan over medium-high heat and pour in the batter. Leave to set for about 2 minutes, then use a spatula to stir and scramble. Keep cooking until the batter starts to stick together, about 5–6 minutes. Break up any large clumps as best you can, so it resembles scrambled eggs, then remove from the wok and set aside, breaking up into smaller clumps if necessary.

Whisk together the tamarind, soy sauce, sugar, lime juice and sriracha to make your pad thai sauce.

Wipe out the wok, then set over medium heat, pour in the rest of the oil and fry the garlic and shallots until fragrant and the shallots have softened, 4–5 minutes. Add the vegetables, pad thai sauce and tofu, then stir to combine. Add the noodles and stir to coat well; if they still seem too crunchy, add about ¼ cup (60 ml) water to steam and soften them further. Toss and fry everything for 3–4 minutes, until the noodles are soft but chewy, and the vegetables are tender. Garnish with peanuts, lime wedges, a handful of bean sprouts and some chopped cilantro.

NOTE If you have more time, prepare the noodles beforehand the way the Thais do: Soak them in cold water for 40–60 minutes until they turn white and are soft and pliable but still slightly crunchy. Drain well. You can either cook the noodles immediately or store them in a sealed plastic bag in the fridge for up to 2 days.

Mushroom tom yum soup

 GF

Use tamari instead of soy sauce.

Serves 4
—
Prep time: 10 minutes
Cooking time: 30 minutes

6 cups (1.5 liters) vegetable stock
2 lemongrass stalks, tender white parts only, thinly sliced
4 makrut lime leaves
1 red chili, seeded and very finely chopped
2 shallots, finely chopped
6 garlic cloves, finely chopped
2 inches (5 cm) galangal or ginger, cut into 1 cm slices
2 cups (180 g) mixed mushrooms, such as button and oyster
1 cup (150 g) cherry tomatoes, halved
½ teaspoon red pepper flakes
2 teaspoons tomato paste
2 teaspoons coconut sugar (or grated palm sugar)
1 tablespoon plus 1 teaspoon light soy sauce
2½ tablespoons lime juice
one 14-ounce (400 g) block extra-firm tofu, pressed (page 25) and cubed
¼ teaspoon salt
cilantro leaves, to garnish

My favorite Thai dish when I was growing up was the tangy and assertive tom yum soup – the broth is perfectly poised between hot and sour, making it irresistible. When making tom yum, never skimp on the aromatics. The soup relies on the lemongrass, galangal, makrut lime leaves and chili to impart a distinctive, herbaceous flavor.

Put all the ingredients except the cilantro in a large saucepan. Bring to a boil, then reduce the heat to low, cover and simmer for 20–30 minutes, until all the flavors have infused and your kitchen smells of lemongrass and ginger.

Serve the soup piping hot, garnished with cilantro.

Thai green curry

GF

Use tamari instead of soy sauce.

Serves 4
—
Prep time: 30 minutes
Cooking time: 30 minutes

Green curry paste
2 lemongrass stalks, white
   parts only, thinly sliced
2 inches (5 cm) ginger or
   galangal, chopped
4 garlic cloves, chopped
3 shallots, chopped
2 green chilies, seeded and
   chopped
1 teaspoon coconut sugar (or
   grated palm sugar)
1 teaspoon ground coriander
½ teaspoon ground cumin
1 tablespoon plus 1 teaspoon
   soy sauce
2½ tablespoons lime juice
1 tablespoon plus 1 teaspoon
   tamarind paste
½ cup (25 g) chopped
   cilantro leaves
½ cup lightly packed (15 g)
   Thai (or regular) basil leaves

1 cup (250 ml) coconut milk
1 cup (250 ml) vegetable stock
2 teaspoons soy sauce
1 teaspoon coconut sugar (or
   grated palm sugar)
2 makrut lime leaves
one 14-ounce (400 g) block
   extra-firm tofu, pressed
   (page 25) and cubed
1 large eggplant, cubed, or
   7–8 baby eggplants, halved
1 large red chili, seeded and
   sliced
½ cup lightly packed (15 g)
   Thai (or regular) basil leaves
steamed jasmine rice, to serve

Thai curries often take a bit more effort than their Indian counterparts, with the requirement to make your own curry paste. While it is difficult to surpass the bright flavors of freshly made green curry paste, you can always use a store-bought version. Just be sure to check the ingredients list, because some contain fish sauce or shrimp paste – and note that you'll only need ¼ cup (55 g), as it will be more concentrated than the one below.

You can make the curry paste with a mortar and pestle, which is ideal, or in a food processor or blender, which is quicker. While using the mortar and pestle takes more elbow grease, it releases a lot of flavor and results in a more aromatic paste. Simply pound or blend all the paste ingredients together until smooth and even, adding a splash of water if necessary, particularly if you are using a food processor. Set the paste aside.

Pour a splash of coconut milk into a large saucepan over medium heat. Add the curry paste and fry for about 4 minutes, stirring often, to release its flavor and aroma. The kitchen should smell amazing at this point! Add the rest of the coconut milk, along with the stock, soy sauce, sugar, lime leaves and tofu. Cover and bring to a boil. Now add the eggplant and chili and cook for 4–5 minutes until the eggplant is tender and buttery.

Remove the curry from the heat and stir in the basil leaves, then serve with steamed jasmine rice.

Pineapple fried rice

 GF *Use tamari instead of soy sauce.*

Serves 4
—
Prep time: 15 minutes
Cooking time: 15 minutes

2½ tablespoons vegetable oil
half 14-ounce (400 g) block
    extra-firm tofu, pressed
    (page 25) and crumbled
¼ teaspoon ground turmeric
¼ teaspoon black salt or
    regular salt
2 garlic cloves, finely chopped
2 scallions, chopped
1 inch (2.5 cm) ginger, finely
    chopped
3 cups (550 g) cooked rice,
    chilled – jasmine rice works
    best
1 tablespoon plus 1 teaspoon
    soy sauce
1 teaspoon sriracha
2 teaspoons sesame oil
1½ cups (240 g) pineapple
    chunks
½ cup (75 g) frozen peas
cilantro leaves and roasted
    cashews, to garnish

This version of fried rice has the classic Thai sweet-and-salty twist. Pineapple might seem like an odd addition to fried rice, but it works. Much less controversial than pineapple on pizza. I love cutting the pineapples in half and, after scooping out their sunny flesh with a spoon, using the hollow shells as serving bowls. This is a genius way of making this uncomplicated dish look impressive.

Pour half the vegetable oil into a wok or nonstick frying pan over medium-high heat and fry the tofu with the turmeric until it looks drier and firmer, like scrambled eggs. Add the black salt, then pour it out onto a plate.

Wipe out the pan with a paper towel. Add the remaining oil and fry the garlic, scallions and ginger until fragrant, about 3 minutes. Add the rice and continue to fry, breaking up any clumps with a spoon or spatula, for 2 minutes.

Stir in the soy sauce, sriracha and sesame oil, then add the pineapple, peas and the scrambled tofu. Make sure everything is well distributed, then let it cook for 2 minutes, to make sure the fried rice is heated right through.

Serve hot, garnished with cilantro leaves and cashews.

Mango summer rolls

Use tamari instead of soy sauce, and a gluten-free version of hoisin sauce.

Serves 4
—
Prep time: 30 minutes
Cooking time: 15 minutes

Tofu marinade
1 inch (2.5 cm) ginger, finely chopped
2½ tablespoons soy sauce
1 tablespoon lime juice
1 teaspoon sriracha
½ teaspoon liquid smoke – optional

1 block (400 g) extra-firm tofu, pressed (page 25) and sliced into batons

Dipping sauce
¼ cup (65 g) or tahini
2½ tablespoons hoisin sauce
½–1 teaspoon sriracha
1 tablespoon lime juice
1–2 tablespoons hot water

2 bundles (3.5 ounces/100 g) dried rice vermicelli noodles
12 rice paper spring roll wrappers
1 mango, flesh only, peeled and cut into strips
4 mint sprigs, leaves only
3 scallions, cut into matchsticks
3 small carrots, grated
½ cup (75 g) roughly chopped roasted peanuts
black and white sesame seeds, for sprinkling

When making my own summer rolls, I make sure they are so robust in flavor that you could enjoy them even without the sauce. Not that you should – the tahini and hoisin dipping sauce here is incredible, an "eat it out of the bowl with a spoon" kind of incredible.

First marinate the tofu. Mix together all the marinade ingredients, add the tofu and leave for 10 minutes, flipping it over halfway through.

Preheat the oven to 350°F (180°C) and grease a baking sheet.

Put the marinated tofu onto the baking sheet and bake for 15 minutes.

Meanwhile, for the dipping sauce, combine all the ingredients, starting with 1 tablespoon water and only adding more if the sauce seems too thick – this will depend on your tahini.

Boil the noodles for 3 minutes, then drain and dunk immediately into a bowl of cold water.

When you're ready to assemble the rolls, drain the noodles. Fill a shallow bowl with lukewarm water. Dip a wrapper into the water for a few seconds, making sure it gets completely submerged.

Lay out the wrapper on a clean countertop or platter and fill with a little bit of everything. Fold over just one side of the wrapper, if you want the mango to peep out, as in the photo, then fold the wrapper up over the filling and roll up as shown opposite.

Serve the summer rolls with the dipping sauce. These make great party food – everyone can assemble their own!

How to make summer rolls

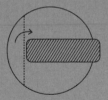

Fold in one edge of the wrapper over the filling – the same applies if your wrapper is a square.

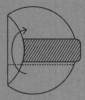

Bring the bottom of the wrapper up and over the filling, keeping it tight.

Roll the filling upwards, wrapping it tightly.

Continuing rolling to form your summer roll, with one end open.

Thai basil "chicken"

Serves 4

—

Prep time: 15 minutes
Cooking time: 10 minutes

1 tablespoon plus 1 teaspoon
  vegetable oil
1 red chili, seeded and finely
  chopped
2 shallots, finely chopped
2 garlic cloves, finely chopped
1 cup (80 g) TVP granules,
  prepared (page 25)
2 teaspoons grated palm sugar
2 teaspoons light soy sauce
2 teaspoons dark soy sauce
1 tablespoon plus 1 teaspoon
  vegetarian oyster sauce
1 cup lightly packed (30 g)
  holy basil or Thai basil
  leaves, plus extra to garnish
steamed jasmine rice and
  lime halves, to serve

Holy Basil was the name of my first food blog, because I adore the taste of this herb. It is different from Italian basil, with a clove-like flavor and mellow menthol aftertaste. Purists will tell you that if you can't use holy basil in basil chicken (*pad krapow gai*), then you shouldn't make it. But vegan cooking is, after all, about adapting and working with what you have. If you can't find holy basil, Thai (or, as a last resort, Italian) basil works well in this dish, even though it won't taste quite so peppery.

Heat the oil in a frying pan over medium heat and fry the chili and shallots until fragrant and the shallots are soft and translucent, about 3 minutes. Stir in the garlic and fry for another 2 minutes.

Now add the drained TVP, sugar, both soy sauces and the oyster sauce. Stir well and leave to cook for 2 minutes. Next, add the basil and cook until it is just wilted. Serve on a bed of hot jasmine rice, garnished with the extra basil leaves and with lime halves for squeezing.

Jackfruit massaman curry

GF

*Use tamari
instead of
soy sauce.*

Serves 4

—

Prep time: 25 minutes
Cooking time: 50 minutes

Massaman curry paste
4 cardamom pods, seeds only
1 tablespoon plus 1 teaspoon
    coriander seeds
1 teaspoon fennel seeds
½ teaspoon cumin seeds
½ teaspoon ground cinnamon
¼ teaspoon ground cloves
¼ teaspoon ground nutmeg
5 garlic cloves, chopped
2 shallots, roughly diced
1 red chili, seeded and chopped
1 inch (2.5 cm) ginger, chopped
1 lemongrass stalk, chopped

1 cup (250 ml) coconut milk
½ cup (125 ml) vegetable stock
2 bay leaves
1 star anise
1 cinnamon stick
1 tablespoon plus 1 teaspoon
    toasted Serundeng (page 22)
4 small waxy potatoes (about
    12 ounces/350 g), steamed
1½ tablespoons grated palm
    sugar
2½ tablespoons tamarind paste
one 20-ounce (565 g) can
    young green jackfruit,
    prepared (page 25)
1 tablespoon plus 1 teaspoon
    light soy sauce
roasted peanuts and sliced red
    chili, to garnish
steamed jasmine rice and lime
    wedges, to serve

Rich and silky, yet somehow quite delicate, massaman curry is actually believed to have Persian roots. The aromatics – cinnamon, cardamom, cloves, and so on – are ground into a paste and then fried in a sizzling pan with coconut milk. This intensifies them and gives the curry a profound depth of flavor. Peanuts are a must, although if you are allergic you can use cashews for a similar nuttiness. Any leftovers make a brilliant packed lunch for the next day.

First, make the curry paste. Toast the cardamom, coriander, fennel and cumin seeds in a dry frying pan over medium heat, stirring often so they don't burn, for about 2 minutes or until fragrant. Transfer to a mortar and pestle and pound to a powder (or use a small blender to do this). Stir in the ground cinnamon, cloves and nutmeg, then add the garlic, shallots, chili, ginger and lemongrass and continue to pound until it forms a paste. (You may need to add a tablespoon or so of water to help with this, especially if you are using a blender.)

Pour about a quarter of the coconut milk into a large wok or saucepan over medium heat. When it's hot, add the curry paste and fry in the coconut milk for about 5 minutes, stirring frequently – this releases the flavor and makes your kitchen smell amazing. It is perfectly okay if your coconut milk starts to split, which tends to happen if you are using the sort with no stabilizers added. In fact, in Thailand, you want the coconut milk to split, as it is considered more authentic!

Now add the rest of the coconut milk, along with the stock, bay leaves, star anise, cinnamon and serundeng. Stir well, then add the potatoes, palm sugar, tamarind and jackfruit. Season with soy sauce, then cover and bring to the boil. Lower the heat to a simmer and cook for about 30 minutes. Finally, stir in the peanuts and cook for 2–3 more minutes.

Taste the curry just before serving, adding a dash more soy sauce or palm sugar to taste, if needed. Garnish with chili slices, then serve with steamed jasmine rice and lime wedges.

Use tamari instead of soy sauce.

Depending on your curry paste . . .

Makes 10

—

Prep time: 20 minutes (plus soaking time)
Cooking time: 20 minutes

one 14-ounce (400 g) can artichokes, drained
¼ cup (40 g) sunflower seeds, soaked in water for 1 hour
2½ tablespoons red curry paste
1 sheet nori, finely shredded
2 scallions, sliced
½ teaspoon light soy sauce
1 inch (2.5 cm) ginger, grated
1 teaspoon lime juice
1 Flax egg (page 21)
½ cup (30 g) panko bread crumbs
2½ tablespoons all-purpose flour

Crispy coating

½ cup (125 ml) plant milk
½ cup (75 g) all-purpose flour
½ cup (30 g) panko bread crumbs
¼ cup (25 g) desiccated coconut
salt and pepper, to taste
vegetable oil, for frying

cilantro sprigs, to garnish

Thai-style ocean cakes

While these do not have the distinctive, springy texture of traditional Thai fish cakes (*tod mun pla*), they taste remarkably briny, with a spicy kick. Remember to check the label when you buy your red curry paste to make sure it doesn't contain any fish sauce or shrimp paste.

Begin by chopping the artichokes finely and placing them in a bowl. Drain the sunflower seeds and blitz in a food processor with the curry paste, nori, scallions, soy sauce, ginger and lime juice. Add to the bowl, along with the Flax egg, bread crumbs and flour. Use a wooden spoon or a fork to combine everything thoroughly.

Now set up a bread-crumbing station: Combine the plant milk and flour in one wide, shallow bowl and the bread crumbs, coconut, salt and pepper in another.

Pour a little oil into a nonstick frying pan and set it over medium heat. Form the mixture into patties about 3 inches (7.5 cm) in diameter. Take a patty, dip it into the flour and milk mixture, then into the bread crumb mixture, pressing in the crumbs. Fry until golden brown on each side, flipping it halfway – it should take 4–5 minutes in total. If you have a large pan, you should be able to fry up to three at a time.

Drain on paper towels, then garnish with cilantro and serve with a side of Cucumber relish (see below).

NOTE If you would prefer to bake these, preheat the oven to 375°F (190°C) and line a baking sheet with parchment paper or a silicone mat. Spray with oil and bake the patties for 15–17 minutes, flipping halfway – note that they will not brown when cooked this way.

Serves 4

—

Prep time: 5 minutes
Cooking time: 10 minutes

¼ cup (60 ml) rice vinegar
½ cup (110 g) white sugar
1 cucumber, diced
2½ tablespoons crushed roasted peanuts
1 small chili, diced

Cucumber relish

This tangy and addictive relish works as a side to many dishes, even pairing perfectly with Satay (page 103).

In a small saucepan over medium heat, add the vinegar and sugar to ¼ cup (60 ml) water. Bring to a boil and let it bubble for about 6 minutes, until the vinegar smell starts to mellow. Add the cucumber, peanuts and chili, stir to coat well and then transfer to a bowl and leave to cool.

Cover and keep in the fridge until ready to serve.

Mushroom laab

GF *Use tamari instead of soy sauce.*

Serves 2 as a starter or side
—
Prep time: 20 minutes
Cooking time: 15 minutes

2½ tablespoons sticky rice or jasmine rice

1½ cups (150 g) sliced oyster mushrooms, or mushroom of choice

2 shallots, thinly sliced

3 scallions, finely chopped

2 mint sprigs, leaves only

2 cilantro sprigs, leaves only – optional

1 tablespoon plus 1 teaspoon lime juice

1 tablespoon plus 1 teaspoon light soy sauce

1 teaspoon grated palm sugar

½–1 teaspoon chili flakes

baby roma (plum) tomatoes, mint sprigs and lime wedges, to serve

Thai salads are among the best in the world – I just love their characteristic interplay of sweet and savory. While green papaya salad will always be my go-to, this mushroom salad (*laab het*) is a close second. It calls for roasted and ground rice, which adds a contrasting crunch and nuttiness and is easy to make at home. For something more substantial, serve this salad alongside steaming clouds of sticky rice. This is also refreshing eaten cold, straight from the fridge – but if serving it cold, only add the roasted rice just before serving or it will go soft and you'll lose that nice contrasting crunchy texture.

First, make the roasted rice. Toast the raw rice in a dry frying pan over high heat for 15 minutes, stirring constantly, until golden – it should smell like popcorn. Remove from the pan and let it cool a little before using a mortar and pestle or spice grinder to grind the rice into a powder that resembles fine sand.

Next, bring a saucepan of water to a boil, add the mushrooms and blanch for 20 seconds. Drain immediately and transfer to a large salad bowl, then add the rest of the ingredients, including the roasted rice you made earlier.

Toss everything together well and serve right away, garnished with halved baby tomatoes, mint sprigs and lime wedges.

Sweet corn fritters

 Use tamari instead
of soy sauce.

 Depending on your
curry paste ...

Makes 20
—
Prep time: 15 minutes
Cooking time: 20 minutes

vegetable oil spray
2 cups (325 g) cooked sweet
 corn kernels, from about 2
 ears
1 Flax egg (page 21)
1 teaspoon light soy sauce
2½ tablespoons red curry
 paste
¼ cup (60 ml) soy milk
¾ cup (125 g) rice flour
¼ teaspoon baking powder
½ cup lightly packed (15 g)
 Thai (or regular) basil
 leaves, chopped
2 scallions, chopped
pinch of black pepper
cilantro leaves and lime
 wedges, to serve

Crispy exterior and slightly chewy center, sweet and salty: Somehow, in these sweet corn fritters (*tod man khao pod*), opposites coexist. Store-bought red curry paste is fine for these – just check the ingredients list to make sure it doesn't contain any fish sauce or shrimp paste.

Preheat the oven to 400°F (200°C). Line a baking sheet with a silicone mat or parchment paper, then spray well with oil.

In a food processor, blend half of the sweet corn kernels with the Flax egg, soy sauce, curry paste, soy milk, flour and baking powder. Process until smooth, then pour into a bowl and fold in the remaining sweet corn, basil leaves, scallion and pepper.

Drop dollops of the batter onto the prepared baking sheet, flattening them out slightly, like cookies. Spray a thin coat of oil on top of the fritters and bake for 10 minutes. Remove from the oven, flip the fritters over, spray with oil and bake for another 10 minutes.

When they're done, the fritters should be golden brown and fragrant. Scatter with cilantro leaves and serve hot, with lime wedges and a small bowl of Thai sweet chili sauce (see below).

Thai sweet chili sauce

Makes about 1 cup (250 ml)
—
Prep time: 5 minutes
Cooking time: 15 minutes

½ cup (175 g) rice syrup
½ cup (175 g) agave syrup
2½ tablespoons rice vinegar
1½ teaspoons salt
2½ tablespoons cornstarch
1 heaped teaspoon red
 pepper flakes
½ teaspoon garlic powder

No one is a stranger to sweet chili sauce. I went through a phase of adding it to my salads every day. However, since a lot of store-bought chili sauces contain fish sauce, here is an easy vegan version you can make yourself.

In a saucepan over medium heat, whisk all the ingredients together with ¼ cup (60 ml) water. Continue to whisk and cook until the sauce boils and thickens, about 10 minutes.

Decant into a clean glass jar and store in the fridge for up to 3 weeks.

Coconut pikelets

 GF

Makes 20

—

Prep time: 30 minutes
Cooking time: 15 minutes

Pancake layer
½ cup (80 g) rice flour
½ cup (125 ml) coconut milk
2½ tablespoons water
¼ teaspoon salt

Custard layer
½ cup (125 ml) coconut milk
1 tablespoon plus 1 teaspoon
   white sugar
2 teaspoons tapioca starch

vegetable oil spray
¼ cup (50 g) cooked sweet
   corn kernels
1 scallion, chopped

These delightful little snacks, called *khanom krok*, teeter between a pancake and a custard. Their base is fried like a crispy crepe and then topped with a filling that is cooked only briefly, so that it remains soft, with a definite wobble. There are special "dimpled" cast iron pans you can get to cook them. If you happen to own one, feel free to use it on the stove (see note below), however, I make mine in the oven using a mini-muffin pan – less traditional maybe, but then you don't have to fork out for any specialized equipment.

Put a 20-hole mini-muffin pan into the oven and preheat the oven to 400°F (200°C). Set a timer for 20 minutes and let the pan heat at the same time as the oven.

Meanwhile, prepare the batter for the layers in two separate bowls: Just whisk together the ingredients for each batter until smooth and lump-free.

When the timer goes off, carefully remove the hot muffin pan from the oven, spray each hole with oil and return to the oven for another 10 minutes.

Now, working quickly and carefully (the pan will be very hot!), drop a tablespoon of the pancake batter into each hole – it should sizzle as it hits the pan. Holding the muffin pan with oven gloves, tilt it to bring the batter up the sides of the pan to form a cuplike shape. Bake for 3–5 minutes, until the pancake layer is set. Then spoon 1 teaspoon of the custard into each hole. Sprinkle with a few slivers of scallion and a few kernels of corn, then bake for 5–7 minutes, until set.

NOTE If you have a pan specially designed for making *khanom krok* (or *ebelskiver* or *takoyaki*), preheat it over a medium-high heat on the stove. When it's hot, pour in the pancake layer and fry for 2 minutes before adding the custard and toppings. Cover and cook on low for 15–20 minutes until set.

Mango sticky rice

Serves 4
—
Prep time: 20 minutes
Cooking time: 25 minutes

1 cup (200 g) sticky (sweet) rice, soaked in water for 2 hours or overnight
1 cup (250 ml) coconut milk
¼ cup (55 g) white sugar
1 pandan leaf, knotted – optional
1 tablespoon rice flour
½ teaspoon salt
2 mangoes, peeled, halved and sliced
toasted sesame seeds and mint sprigs, to garnish

Remember what I said about tom yum being my favorite Thai dish? Well, this is my favorite Thai dessert. Slippery slices of fresh mango and creamy glutinous rice, flooded with a salty coconut sauce reminiscent of salted caramel. If you've never had this before, sit tight. You're in for a treat!

Prepare a steamer basket by lining it with cheesecloth and setting it over a saucepan of boiling water. Drain the sticky rice and place it in the steamer basket, bringing the sides of the cloth over the rice to wrap it completely. Cover and steam for 10–15 minutes, until the rice is cooked through – it should still by slightly gummy.

While the rice steams, put the coconut milk and sugar and pandan leaf, if using, in a small saucepan over medium heat. Bring to a boil and stir until the sugar has dissolved, then remove from the heat.

When your rice is done, transfer it into a heatproof bowl. Pour half of the coconut milk mixture over it, then cover and leave it to absorb the liquid. Add the rice flour and salt to the remaining coconut milk mixture in the pan. Put it back over medium heat and stir constantly until the sauce has thickened.

To serve, place half a mango on each plate. Spoon some rice alongside and drizzle with the coconut sauce. Garnish with toasted sesame seeds and a mint sprig, then eat up!

Steamed cupcakes

 GF

Makes 6 small cupcakes
—
**Prep time: 30 minutes
(plus proofing time)
Cooking time: 15 minutes**

¼ cup (55 g) white sugar
½ teaspoon active dry yeast
¼ cup (60 ml) warm water
¼ cup (60 ml) coconut milk
¾ cup (125 g) rice flour
½ teaspoon baking powder
½ teaspoon jasmine extract,
   rose water or vanilla extract,
   or ¼ teaspoon pandan
   extract
few drops of food coloring –
   optional
brown sugar, for dipping

These steamed cupcakes (*khanom pui fai*) come in vibrant colors and, as they cook, they "smile" by bursting open at the top, like a crown. This "smiling" is meant to symbolize growth, making them an auspicious Thai treat to serve when there is something to celebrate. The batter is usually spiked with jasmine extract – just a splash – to add an exotic note. But rose water, vanilla or pandan extract will also work. This recipe only makes a small amount, as all the cupcakes need to fit in the steamer and should really be eaten right away. You can double the recipe if you have a larger steamer and more hungry people to feed!

In a medium-sized bowl, whisk the sugar and yeast into the warm water. Set aside until frothy, about 5 minutes.

Stir in the coconut milk and sift in the rice flour and baking powder. Whisk until you have a smooth, lump-free batter, then cover and let it sit on the counter in a warm place until doubled in size, at least 1 hour.

When the batter is ready, set a steamer basket over a saucepan of boiling water. Add the extract – and food coloring, if using – to the batter, and mix to incorporate.

Find six small heat-resistant teacups. (Waxed paper mini-muffin liners will also work, but it's best to double them up as they can get soggy in the steam.) Pour the batter into the cups and immediately set them in the steamer basket. Place a kitchen towel between the steamer and its lid, stretching it taut and taking care to keep the ends away from the heat. This helps to soak up any condensation, so your cupcakes don't get waterlogged.

Steam the cupcakes for 15 minutes – without lifting the lid, as this can cause them not to "smile."

Serve warm, with a small bowl of brown sugar for dipping. These are best eaten fresh and shouldn't be kept for longer than a day.

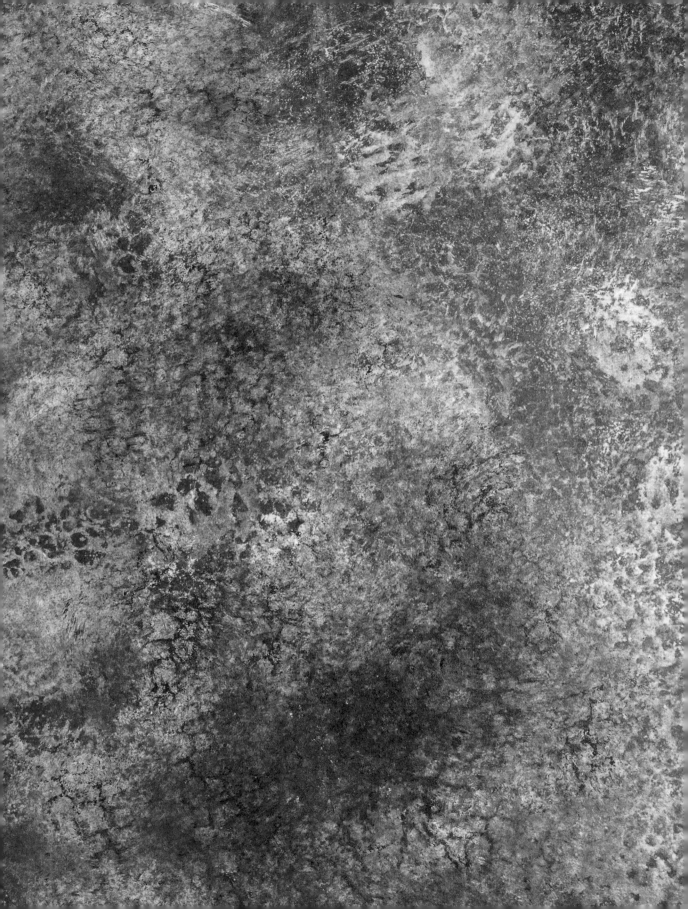

03
Singapore & Malaysia

While the food here is diverse, you would not be the first to notice the similarities between Singaporean and Malaysian cuisine. Perhaps this is due to their close proximity, or to their shared history. Of course, each country claims that their dishes reign supreme and, since both places are home to passionate foodies, the debate is ongoing. The undeniable overlap between the two is the reason they share a chapter in this book: the best of both worlds.

Travel around Singapore and something quickly becomes apparent. In this buzzing place, where quaint, pastel-colored shops are juxtaposed with skyscrapers that kiss the clouds, food is kind of a big deal. Singaporeans just love food – and they *really* love talking about it. The hottest topic is always where you can go to get the best *kaya* toast, or the perfect way to eat a plate of chicken rice.

This street-food mecca is a gastro-tourist's heaven – but somewhat paradoxically, "street food" isn't actually sold on the streets. Instead, hawkers sell their satay skewers and *laksa* noodles in large open-air food courts, aptly named "hawker centers." These hawker centers, where tables are reserved with little packets of tissue paper and strangers nurse their *kopi* (coffee) cheek by jowl, represent the soul of Singaporean food. The food served in these places is a patchwork of cuisines from every corner of Asia. Such cooking may be humble and unflashy, but it is not to be underestimated. The best bowl of noodle soup I have ever had was in a hawker center, as I sat amid the humid, frantic throng of people lining up to nab a carton of sweet bean curd. Eating in Singapore is an experience like no other.

If you spend any length of time in neighboring Malaysia, a word you will soon pick up is *makan*. To *makan* is to eat, and eating is the lifeblood of Malaysian culture. Here, it is not unusual to eat six or seven times in a day. And why not? Otherwise, there just isn't enough time to sample all that Malaysia has to offer – from thick, fragrant *rendang* curries to wedges of fluffy pancake sandwiched with sugary peanuts.

Satay

Use tamari instead of soy sauce.

Makes about 24 skewers
—
Prep time: 1 hour (plus marinating time)
Cooking time: 30 minutes

3 cups (75 g) TVP chunks, prepared (page 25)

Marinade
1 inch (2.5 cm) ginger, finely chopped
2 lemongrass stalks, finely chopped
1 teaspoon ground turmeric
2 teaspoons ground coriander
2 teaspoons ground cumin
¼ cup plus 1 tablespoon (65 g) coconut sugar
¼ cup (60 ml) light soy sauce

Satay sauce
1 teaspoon vegetable oil
1 large shallot, finely chopped
1 stalk lemongrass, finely chopped
2 large garlic cloves, finely chopped
½ teaspoon ground coriander
¼ teaspoon ground cumin
¼ teaspoon fennel seeds
1 large chili, seeded and finely chopped
2½ tablespoons coconut sugar
2 teaspoons tamarind paste
1 tablespoon plus 1 teaspoon light soy sauce
1¼ cups (310 ml) coconut milk
1 cup (140 g) ground roasted peanuts
1 tablespoon plus 1 teaspoon crunchy peanut butter

Compressed rice (page 20), lime halves and cucumber slices, to serve

There used to be a "satay man" who would cycle down our street in the heavy, languid hour just before sunset, with a tiny grill strapped on top of his back wheel. On those glorious days when we were far too lazy to cook, we would flag him down and order two dozen skewers. He would grill them on the spot, filling the air with the ethereal scent of caramelization and bubbling, savory peanut sauce. Satay sauce is – dare I say it – even better than eating peanut butter out of the jar.

In a large bowl, whisk together all the marinade ingredients. Add the drained TVP chunks and mix well to coat. Cover the bowl and leave in the fridge to marinate for 1–4 hours – the longer, the better. Soak 24 wooden skewers in a bowl of cold water (this will keep them from burning on the hot grill pan or barbecue later).

Meanwhile, make the satay sauce. Heat the oil in a large nonstick saucepan over medium-high heat and fry the shallot, lemongrass and garlic until fragrant and soft, about 3 minutes. Add the spices and chili and continue to fry another 3 minutes. Next, stir in the sugar, tamarind and soy sauce and mix well before pouring in the coconut milk. Lower the heat and gently bring to a simmer, then cook for 5 minutes, taking care not to let it boil as this can cause the coconut milk to split and become oily. Stir in the peanuts and peanut butter and keep cooking over low heat, stirring frequently, until the sauce reaches your desired thickness. I usually go for about 4 minutes for a runny but firm sauce – perfect for satay!

Heat a barbecue or grill pan to high heat. Use a skewer to pierce a TVP chunk and then keep threading them along the skewer to form "kebabs" until all the chunks have run out – I usually aim for four or five chunks per skewer. Cook the satay skewers for 3–4 minutes on each side, using a pair of tongs to turn them, until golden brown all over and flecked with darker brown crispy bits.

Serve them right off the grill with compressed rice, lime halves, some cucumber slices for freshness, and the peanut sauce on the side.

Fluffy peanut pancake

Makes 1 big pancake about
9 inches (24 cm) across
(enough for 4)
—
Prep time: 20 minutes
(plus batter-resting time)
Cooking time: 10 minutes

Pancake
1 cup (120 g) sifted
  all-purpose flour
¼ teaspoon baking soda
1 teaspoon active dry yeast
1 Flax egg (page 21)
2½ tablespoons white sugar
¾ cup (185 ml) warm plant
  milk
2 teaspoons vegetable oil
½ teaspoon vanilla extract

Sweet peanut filling
½ cup (65 g) finely chopped
  roasted peanuts
2 tablespoons white sugar

A pancake like you've never had before, *apam balik* has a honeycomb-like texture, with glittering, sugary peanuts nestled inside. Because this is a yeasted batter, it requires some resting time. But instead of spending this time getting impatient, just make the batter before bed and let it ferment overnight. Be warned, though – you will dream of clouds of peanut-adorned pancakes all night long. . . .

Whisk all the pancake ingredients together to make a smooth and lump-free batter. Cover and refrigerate for at least 5 hours, or overnight.

When you're ready to cook, take the batter out of the fridge and let it come to room temperature.

For the sweet peanut filling, mix together the peanuts and sugar and set aside.

Lightly grease a 9-inch (24 cm) nonstick frying pan and place over medium heat. Whisk the pancake batter until smooth – this will cause it to deflate but that's okay! When the pan is hot, pour all the pancake batter into the pan and spread it out into an even circle covering the whole base of the pan and coming slightly up the sides, too. Cook until bubbles form and do not disappear, and the surface is beginning to set, 3–5 minutes.

Sprinkle the peanut filling generously over half of the pancake and cover the pan with a lid. Continue to cook until the top of the pancake is completely set and the bottom is a lovely golden-brown.

Fold the pancake in half, remove from the pan and slice into four wedges. Serve warm.

GF

Serves 4
—

Prep time: 30 minutes
Cooking time: 50 minutes

1¼ cups (250 g) basmati rice
1 bay leaf
2 cardamom pods, crushed
½ cinnamon stick
3 cloves
½ teaspoon salt

Fried onions

2 tablespoons vegetable oil
1 large white onion, sliced
¼ cup (45 g) golden raisins
¼ cup (40 g) cashews
¼ teaspoon salt

Curry

1 tablespoon vegetable oil
1 large white onion, sliced
5 cardamom pods, crushed
½ cinnamon stick
5 cloves
½ teaspoon chili powder
1 teaspoon ground coriander
½ teaspoon ground turmeric
1 bay leaf
¼ teaspoon black pepper
2 large tomatoes, pureed, or
   ½ cup (125 ml) passata
1 chili, very finely chopped
½ cup (130 g) vegan yogurt
1 cup (140 g) frozen peas
1 cup (155 g) chopped carrots
1 cup (150 g) sliced green
   beans
one 20-ounce (565 g) can
   young green jackfruit,
   prepared (page 25)
1½ cups (375 ml) vegetable
   stock
1 teaspoon salt

¼ cup (15 g) chopped mint
¼ cup (15 g) chopped cilantro
¼ cup plus 1 tablespoon
   (75 ml) plant milk
½ teaspoon ground turmeric

Jackfruit biryani

While the origins of biryani can be traced back to Persia or India, *dum biryani* is a variation that is especially popular in Malaysia and Singapore. It involves layering the rice and curry in a large pot, then scattering it with herbs before sealing it and letting it cook in its own fragrant steam.

Place the rice, bay leaf, cardamom pods, cinnamon stick, cloves and salt in a saucepan with 2½ cups (625 ml) water. Bring to a boil, then cover, lower the heat and simmer until the rice is three-quarters cooked, about 10 minutes. Remove the bay leaf and spices, and set the rice aside.

Now for the fried onions. Heat the oil in a large saucepan over medium-high heat and fry the onions until wilted and lightly golden, stirring constantly to prevent them from burning. This could take up to 10 minutes, but watch them closely. Add the raisins and cashews and continue to fry until the cashews start to brown, about 5 minutes. Transfer onto a plate lined with paper towels and set aside.

In the same saucepan, make the curry. Place the pan over medium heat, add the oil and fry the onion until translucent and fragrant, about 4 minutes. Add all the spices, together with the bay leaf and pepper. Stir to coat the onion in the spices, then add the tomatoes and chili. Let it bubble away until the tomatoes have thickened slightly and are saucy, about 4 minutes. Stir in the yogurt, all the vegetables, jackfruit, stock and salt. Cover and cook for 5 minutes or until the carrots and beans are three-quarters done – they should still be slightly crunchy.

Now it is time to layer your biryani. This works best in a heavy-bottomed flameproof casserole or Dutch oven, but a large saucepan will also do the trick. Spoon the curry into the base, then spread the rice out evenly on top, flattening it down as best you can. Sprinkle the fried onion mixture over the rice, then scatter some of the mint and cilantro leaves on top. Mix the plant milk and turmeric together and drizzle it over the top, dying patches of the rice yellow – this will create a beautiful marbled effect later. Cover with a tight-fitting lid and cook over low heat for 7–10 minutes, by which time the rice should be lovely and tender. Serve piping hot, garnished with the remaining cilantro and mint.

NOTE Instead of the vegan yogurt, you could use soured soy milk: Place 2 teaspoons lemon juice in a ½ cup (125 ml) measuring cup and top with soy milk. Set aside for about 15 minutes to let it curdle.

Laksa lemak

Serves 4
—
Prep time: 25 minutes
Cooking time: 20 minutes

Laksa paste
2 lemongrass stalks, white parts
  only, chopped
7 small shallots, chopped
1 inch (2.5 cm) ginger or
  galangal, chopped
6 red chilies, seeded and
  chopped
6 garlic cloves, chopped
7 macadamia nuts
  (or 12 cashews)
1 teaspoon ground turmeric
1 tablespoon plus 1 teaspoon
  miso paste

4 cups (1 liter) vegetable stock
1 tablespoon plus 1 teaspoon
  tamarind paste (or 2½
  tablespoons lime juice)
1 tablespoon plus 1 teaspoon
  coconut sugar (or grated palm
  sugar)
¼ cup (40 g) Serundeng (page
  22)
7 tofu puffs or one 14-ounce
  (400 g) block extra-firm tofu,
  cubed
1 cup (180 g) baby corn, halved
1½ cups (90 g) enoki or button
  mushrooms
28 ounces (800 g) fresh laksa
  noodles, or 10.5 ounces (300 g)
  dried rice vermicelli noodles
1½ cups (375 ml) coconut milk
5 scallions, thinly sliced
1 red chili, sliced
1 cup (115 g) bean sprouts
¼ cup (15 g) chopped cilantro
2 limes, cut in half

Lemak means "creamy," here referring to the coconut milk that enriches the laksa and makes it meltingly smooth and velvety. If you cannot find traditional laksa noodles for this dish, you can use either rice vermicelli noodles, udon noodles, or even a mix of the two.

First make the laksa paste. Using a food processor or mortar and pestle, blitz or pound all the ingredients together until smooth.

Pour the stock into a large saucepan over medium heat, then add the tamarind paste, coconut sugar, serundeng and the laksa paste. Stir to mix well, bring to a boil and leave to cook for 5 minutes. Add the tofu puffs, baby corn and mushrooms. Cover and bring back to a boil.

Meanwhile, prepare the noodles. If using dried noodles, place in a pan of boiling water and cook for 7 minutes, then drain and immediately plunge them into a bowl of ice-cold water. If using fresh noodles, just dunk them in boiling water for about 1 minute to loosen, then drain and set aside.

Once the baby corn is cooked through, lower the heat and pour in the coconut milk. Return the soup to a simmer, but be careful not to let it boil or the coconut milk will split.

To serve, divide the drained noodles between four bowls. Ladle the soup into the bowls, then garnish with scallions, chili, bean sprouts, cilantro and a lime half. Slurp up!

Malaysian rojak salad

**Serves 2 as a main,
or 4 as a side**
—
**Prep time: 20 minutes
Cooking time: no cooking
needed**

Dressing
1 tablespoon plus 1 teaspoon
   hoisin sauce
1 teaspoon dark soy sauce
1 teaspoon dark brown sugar
1 tablespoon plus 1 teaspoon
   tamarind paste
1 teaspoon toasted sesame
   seeds
finely grated zest of 1 small
   lime

2 tofu puffs
½ cup (100 g) small
   pineapple chunks
½ cup (100 g) small jicama or
   turnip cubes
¼ cup (50 g) small cucumber
   cubes
¼ cup (40 g) small green
   apple chunks
¼ cup (20 g) bean sprouts,
   blanched
2 tablespoons sesame seeds
2 tablespoons crushed
   roasted peanuts

It feels like a great injustice to call this a fruit salad, because *oh,* it is so much more. Chunks of fruit, vegetable and crispy tofu pieces are drowned in a sticky, syrupy dressing. Taste it frequently as you go along, adjusting as necessary. The mark of a good *rojak* is this dressing, so it's important to get it just right. The beauty of this dish lies in the ability to swap out the ingredients in it according to what you like, making it a great way to use up any flagging fruit and veg in your crisper drawer. Hate pineapples? Use some ripe jackfruit. Not a fan of cucumber? Then use more jicama. Just aim for about 2 cups, or 250 g, of fruit and veg total.

First make the dressing. In a small bowl, combine all the ingredients and mix until smooth.

Toast the tofu puffs under a hot broiler for a minute or two, then use a pair of scissors to cut them up into chunks. Put the tofu puffs in a large bowl, then add the pineapple, jicama, cucumber, green apple and bean sprouts. Drizzle over the dressing and toss well to coat.

Sprinkle with the sesame seeds and peanuts, then serve.

Popiah spring rolls

Makes 8 (enough for 4)
—
Prep time: 35 minutes
Cooking time: 20 minutes

one 14-ounce (400 g) block extra-firm tofu, pressed (page 25) and cubed
1 cup (115 g) bean sprouts
1 head of lettuce or 1 bag baby spinach
½ cup (70 g) roasted peanuts
8 wheat spring roll wrappers
hoisin sauce and Sambal (page 121) or sriracha, to serve

Stewed vegetable filling
1 tablespoon plus 1 teaspoon vegetable oil
1 white onion, finely sliced
3 garlic cloves, very finely chopped
1 tablespoon plus 1 teaspoon miso paste
1 small jicama or kohlrabi, peeled and shredded
2 tablespoons light soy sauce
1 large carrot, grated

The Singaporean answer to a taco party begins with popiah. Think of it as the burrito of Singapore, plump with a glistening tangle of stewed jicama, inky-black sweet sauce and a dazzling array of other ingredients. The next time you feel daunted by the thought of entertaining, simply stew some jicama in a large pot until it collapses and turns salty-sweet. Set out the other fillings in deep bowls and let your guests take care of the assembly. Taco Party 2.0.

First make the filling. Pour the oil into a large saucepan over medium-high heat and fry the onion and garlic until fragrant, and the onions are soft and translucent, about 3 minutes. Add the miso paste, jicama, soy sauce and carrot. Cover, lower the heat and cook until the vegetables are soft and very tender, about 10–15 minutes.

Meanwhile, prepare all the other ingredients. Lightly pan-fry the tofu in a nonstick pan with some oil until golden, rinse and drain the bean sprouts, rinse and dry the lettuce or spinach, and grind the peanuts.

When the filling is cooked, you can begin to make the popiah. Lay out a spring roll wrapper and place a lettuce leaf on top. Top with a large spoonful of the filling, then add a few cubes of tofu, a handful of bean sprouts and some peanuts. Drizzle with hoisin sauce and sambal or sriracha, if desired, then tuck the edges and roll it up tightly (see opposite). The tighter you make the roll, the easier it will be to eat without it falling apart! At home, we like to spread everything out on the table so everyone can assemble their own.

How to make spring rolls

Fold the edges of the circle in, over the filling – the same applies if your wrapper is a square.

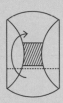

Bring the bottom of the wrapper up and over the filling, keeping it tight.

Roll the filling upward, tucking it in tightly.

Continue rolling to form your spring roll.

Nasi lemak

Serves 4
—

Prep time: 30 minutes
Cooking time: 20 minutes

1½ cups (300 g) jasmine rice
2 pandan leaves, knotted (or
   2 bay leaves)
1 lemongrass stalk, bruised
½ teaspoon salt
¾ cup (185 ml) coconut milk

Vegetable stir-fry
1 teaspoon vegetable oil
1 garlic clove, finely chopped
1 cup (125 g) green beans, cut
   into 1-inch (2.5 cm) lengths
1 large carrot, cut into thin
   strips
¼ teaspoon salt

Tofu scramble
1 teaspoon vegetable oil
½ 14-ounce (400 g) block
   extra-firm tofu, pressed
   (page 25) and crumbled
pinch of black salt
1 tablespoon plus 1 teaspoon
   nutritional yeast – optional
pinch of ground turmeric
pinch of black pepper

1 cup (140 g) roasted peanuts
Sambal (page 121), to serve
1 cucumber, sliced

This is a traditional Malaysian breakfast, although it's equally delicious for lunch or dinner. Rice is enriched with coconut milk and herbaceous pandan, and then eaten with peanuts, vegetables and fiery Sambal. If you're tempted to transform it into a truly sumptuous meal, Tempeh rendang (page 120) makes a fabulous accompaniment!

Put the rice in a saucepan with the pandan leaves, lemongrass, salt, coconut milk and 1½ cups (375 ml) water. Set over medium-high heat and stir, then bring to a boil, cover and reduce the heat to low. Cook until the rice is tender and no more liquid remains, about 15 minutes.

Meanwhile, make the vegetable stir-fry. Put the oil in a nonstick frying pan over medium heat, add the garlic and fry until fragrant, about 1 minute. Add the green beans, carrot and salt. Add ¼ cup (60 ml) water, cover and cook until the vegetables are tender and all the water has evaporated. Set aside.

Wipe out the pan with a paper towel, ready to make the tofu scramble. Put the oil in the pan and set over medium heat, then add the tofu, black salt, nutritional yeast, turmeric and pepper. Stir to mix together well, then cook for about 3 minutes.

To serve, put a large spoonful of rice on each plate. Place some of the stir-fry and the tofu alongside, then sprinkle roasted peanuts on the plate. Finish with a dollop of sambal and cucumber slices to help cut through the heat.

Use tamari in place of soy sauce, and two blocks of well-pressed tofu (page 25) instead of seitan "chicken."

Serves 4

—

Prep time: 50 minutes (plus marinating time)
Cooking time: 50 minutes

2 tofu puffs
1 Seitan "chicken" (page 22)
1½ cups (300 g) long-grain rice, rinsed and drained
1 pandan leaf, knotted (or ½ lemongrass stalk, bruised)
1 inch (2.5 cm) ginger, finely grated
1 teaspoon white sugar
2 tablespoons light soy sauce
2 inches (5 cm) ginger, thinly sliced
½ teaspoon sesame oil
1 small cucumber, sliced

Marinade

2 teaspoons agave syrup
1 teaspoon five spice powder
½ teaspoon molasses
2 inches (5 cm) ginger, finely chopped
2½ tablespoons light soy sauce
pinch of white pepper

Soup

1 teaspoon vegetable oil
4 garlic cloves, finely chopped
2 inches (5 cm) ginger, finely chopped
4 scallions, green parts only, finely chopped
2 dried shiitake mushrooms
1 teaspoon Chicken-style seasoning (page 20) or nutritional yeast
½ teaspoon salt

Hainanese chili sauce

2 large red chilies, seeded and chopped
2 garlic cloves, chopped
1 teaspoon salt
1 tablespoon plus 1 teaspoon lemon juice

Hainanese "chicken" rice

There is something quite beautiful about the simplicity of this dish, widely considered the national dish of Singapore.

Cut along the sides of the tofu puffs and roll each one flat to form a long sheet of tofu skin. Place a flattened tofu puff on top of each seitan log and stretch it across to cover the top, using toothpicks to hold it in place and form a "skin" on your seitan "chicken." Combine all the marinade ingredients in a bowl and add the seitan "chicken," mixing well. Cover and chill for 1 hour, flipping it over halfway through.

Preheat the oven to 350°F (175°C) and oil a small baking sheet. Transfer the marinated "chicken" onto the sheet and brush with some of the marinade from the bowl, reserving about 1 tablespoon for a final baste. Bake for 10 minutes, then remove from the oven, brush on the remaining marinade and bake for a further 15 minutes.

For the soup, put the vegetable oil in a large saucepan over medium heat and fry the garlic, ginger and scallion until fragrant, 2–3 minutes. Pour in 6 cups (1.5 liters) water, then add the mushrooms, chicken-style seasoning and salt. Bring to a boil, then simmer for 30 minutes, to infuse the soup with all the lovely umami flavors from the shiitakes. Discard the mushrooms, then pour all but 2 cups (500 ml) of the soup into a heatproof bowl and reserve for later.

Add the rice to the remaining soup in the pan, along with the pandan leaf and grated ginger. Bring to a boil, then reduce the heat to medium-low, cover and cook for a further 12–15 minutes, until the rice is tender and cooked.

Meanwhile, dissolve the sugar in 1 tablespoon plus 1 teaspoon hot water, then mix in the soy sauce to make a dipping sauce. Simmer the sliced ginger in a little water for 5 minutes to soften. Drain and blitz in a blender, adding a splash of water if necessary, to make a ginger sauce.

To make the chili sauce, put the chili and garlic in a small saucepan of boiling water and cook for 5 minutes. Drain, then transfer to a small food processor or blender. Add the salt and lemon juice and blitz everything together.

To serve, brush the seitan "chicken" with the sesame oil, then remove the toothpicks and slice. Place some sliced "chicken" on each plate and add a large spoonful of rice, some of the sliced cucumber, ginger and chili sauces, with a bowl of black dipping sauce on the side. Remember the extra soup you set aside? Serve that too, in little bowls, for slurping up in between mouthfuls of fragrant rice.

Tempeh rendang

Serves 4
—

Prep time: 20 minutes
Cooking time: 30 minutes

¼ cup (25 g) desiccated
   coconut
4 garlic cloves, roughly
   chopped
3 shallots, roughly chopped
1 inch (2.5 cm) ginger,
   roughly chopped
1 lemongrass stalk, white part
   only, roughly chopped
1 teaspoon ground coriander
1 teaspoon ground cumin
1 teaspoon ground turmeric
½ teaspoon ground cinnamon
1 teaspoon grated palm sugar
   (or brown sugar)
½ teaspoon salt
½ cup (125 ml) coconut milk
2 teaspoons tamarind paste
1 star anise
2 cloves
one 8-ounce (227 g) block
   tempeh, sliced

Rendang is not, strictly speaking, a curry. It does not come swimming in gravy, but is instead quite thick – rich with coconut and sharp from the tamarind. While this is often partnered with Nasi lemak (page 115), you can also enjoy it with Compressed rice (page 20) and Sambal (opposite).

In a nonstick frying pan over medium heat, dry-fry the coconut until it is brown and fragrant. Transfer to a food processor or blender and add the garlic, shallots, ginger, lemongrass, ground spices, sugar, salt, coconut milk, tamarind and ½ cup (125 ml) water. Blitz everything together to make a smooth sauce.

Pour into a saucepan over medium-high heat and add the star anise, cloves and tempeh. Bring to a boil, then lower the heat and simmer gently for 10–15 minutes before serving. For a thicker rendang, continue to simmer and reduce for another 10 minutes.

Sambal

Use a gluten-free miso paste.

Prep time: 20 minutes
Cooking time: 15 minutes

7–8 large red chilies
   (3.5 ounces/100 g in total),
   seeded and thinly sliced
1 tablespoon plus 1 teaspoon
   miso paste
1½ teaspoons grated palm
   sugar (or brown sugar)
1 tablespoon plus 1 teaspoon
   tamarind paste
1 shallot, chopped
2 garlic cloves, finely chopped
2 macadamia nuts
   (or 4 cashews)
1 tablespoon plus 1 teaspoon
   vegetable oil

Sambal is a lip-tingling, deep crimson chili paste. It has, dare I say it, a similar flavor profile to sriracha (heavy on the garlic, with a tinge of sweetness), but with a black-belt karate kick. My nana's version relies on dried chilies, which can be difficult to find, so this recipe uses the fresh kind. When choosing chilies for this recipe, avoid smaller ones, such as bird's eye chilies, as they can be wickedly hot and it would be a hassle to seed them all.

Using a mortar and pestle or small food processor, blend the chilies, miso, sugar, tamarind, shallot, garlic and macadamia nuts to a smooth paste – you may need to add a few tablespoons of water to help with this, but use as little as possible, adding a tablespoon at a time.

Heat the oil in a small saucepan over low heat, add the paste and fry, stirring constantly, until it is fragrant and has become darker and less watery – this should take around 15 minutes. Let it cool, then transfer to a sterilized glass jar and store in the fridge. It should keep for about a month.

NOTE If you can take some heat, leave in the seeds of one or two of the chilies. But be warned, two really is the maximum here; beyond that it can get painfully spicy!

Char kuey teow

Use tamari instead of light and dark soy sauce, and make your own Kecap manis (page 21) from tamari as well. Leave out the vegetarian oyster sauce, or use the mushroom-cooking liquid in its place, as described on page 14.

Serves 4

—

Prep time: 20 minutes
Cooking time: 15 minutes

1 pound (450 g) fresh flat rice noodles or 7 ounces (200 g) dried flat rice noodles
1 tablespoon vegetable oil
half 14-ounce (400 g) block extra-firm tofu, pressed (page 25) and crumbled
4 garlic cloves, finely chopped
1 inch (2.5 cm) ginger, finely chopped
1 vegetable bouillon cube
½ cup (60 g) sliced oyster mushrooms
1 cup (90 g) shredded napa cabbage or savoy cabbage
1 cup (50 g) shredded greens, such as choy sum, bok choy or Swiss chard, any coarse stems removed
½ cup (20 g) sliced chives or scallions
1½ cups (150 g) bean sprouts
2½ tablespoons light soy sauce
2½ tablespoons dark soy sauce
2½ tablespoons vegetarian oyster sauce
¼ cup (60 ml) Kecap manis (page 21)
Sambal (page 121) and lime wedges, to serve

These stir-fried Penang-style noodles are incredibly popular in both Malaysia and Singapore. *Char kuey teow* may not be very handsome, but look beyond appearances and these glistening noodles are just heavenly – all languid and smoky. If you can't find the wide kuey teow rice noodles traditionally used for this, just opt for the slightly thinner rice noodles that are often used for pad thai. Make sure all your ingredients are ready to go before you start to cook: Once you start stir-frying, you can't stop!

If using fresh noodles, blanch them in a saucepan of boiling water to loosen them – they will only need about 30 seconds or so. If using dried noodles, pour boiling water from a kettle into a heatproof bowl and soak the noodles for 4–7 minutes. Either way, the noodles should still be a little crunchy, as you will be cooking them further in the wok. Drain and rinse well under cold running water to get rid of any excess starch and keep them from getting sticky, then set aside.

Pour about half the oil into a wok or large frying pan over high heat and fry the tofu for 5 minutes, or until it is starting to brown ever so slightly. Set aside. Pour in the rest of the oil, then stir-fry the garlic and ginger until fragrant and golden. Add the bouillon cube and break it up to dissolve. Add the mushrooms and fry for a minute before adding the cabbage, greens, chives and all except ½ cup (50 g) of the bean sprouts and stir-fry until just wilted.

Make a well in the center and add the soy sauces, oyster sauce and kecap manis. Stir in the fried tofu. Continue to mix and combine until everything is well coated. Add the rice noodles and stir to combine. Finally, for extra crunch, stir in the reserved bean sprouts and cook for 1 minute.

Serve immediately with sambal and lime wedges. Enjoy it while it's hot!

Prep time: 30 minutes

Cooking time: 30 minutes

Cookie dough

¼ cup (50 g) vegan butter, softened

1 tablespoon plus 1 teaspoon
   aquafaba (page 11)

¾ cup (100 g) all-purpose flour,
   sifted

¼ cup (55 g) white sugar

1 tablespoon custard powder (or
   cornstarch plus 1 teaspoon vanilla
   extract)

¼ teaspoon baking powder

½ teaspoon vanilla extract

¼ teaspoon almond extract

drop of yellow food coloring –
   optional

Bun dough

½ cup (125 ml) lukewarm water

¼ cup (60 ml) coconut milk

¼ cup (60 ml) aquafaba

2½ tablespoons white sugar

1 packet (2½ teaspoons) active dry
   yeast

2½ tablespoons vegetable oil

2½ cups (375 g) all-purpose flour

¼ teaspoon salt

"Char siew" filling

1 tablespoon plus 1 teaspoon
   vegetable oil

1 white onion, diced

1 tablespoon plus 1 teaspoon dark
   soy sauce

2 teaspoons white sugar

1 teaspoon sesame oil

1 tablespoon plus 1 teaspoon hoisin
   sauce

¾ cup (60 g) TVP chunks, prepared
   (page 25), drained and cut in half

pinch of white pepper

1 teaspoon all-purpose flour

Glaze

2½ tablespoons plant milk

2 teaspoons agave syrup

"Char siew" polo buns

Why are these called "polo" buns, you ask? Well, it's a corruption of the Cantonese *bo lo*, which means pineapple – their mottled golden glaze crackles in the oven, making them look a little like a pineapple.

First, make the cookie dough. In a large bowl, cream the butter until pale and creamy, about 3 minutes. Add the remaining ingredients and mix well: It may seem dry at first but will soon form a stiff dough. Shape into a log, cover with plastic wrap and refrigerate until firm, about 1 hour.

Next, the bun dough. Put the lukewarm water, coconut milk, aquafaba and sugar in a large bowl. Whisk to combine, then sprinkle in the yeast and whisk again. Set aside until frothy, about 10 minutes. Stir in the oil, then gradually sift in the flour and salt. Mix with a wooden spoon until it starts to come together, then turn out onto a clean countertop and knead to a smooth, elastic dough, about 7 minutes. Return it to the bowl and cover with a damp kitchen towel. Set aside in a warm place until doubled in size, about 1 hour.

Now for the "char siew" filling. Heat the oil in a large nonstick frying pan over medium-high heat and fry the onion until translucent, about 3 minutes. Add the soy sauce, sugar, sesame oil and hoisin sauce. Stir in the TVP chunks and fry for another 2–3 minutes, then add the white pepper. Whisk the flour with ¼ cup (60 ml) water until smooth, then add to the pan and cook, stirring constantly, until the filling thickens. Leave to cool while you shape the buns.

Punch the risen bun dough with your fist to knock it back, then turn out onto a well-floured countertop and divide into 10 pieces. Use a rolling pin to roll each one into a circle 5–6 inches (13–15 cm) across, then place a heaped tablespoon of filling in the middle. Pinch the dough together at the top, completely enclosing the filling. When all the buns are rolled and filled, remove the cookie dough from the fridge and divide into ten. Take a cookie dough ball and cover with plastic wrap, then roll out into a circle about 5 mm thick and wide enough to cover the top of a bun. Place on the bun and score in a criss-cross "pineapple" pattern.

Once all the buns are topped with cookie dough, transfer to a baking sheet lined with parchment paper. Make the glaze by whisking the plant milk and agave syrup together. Brush over the tops of the buns, cover with plastic wrap and leave in a warm place to rise for 20 minutes.

Meanwhile, preheat the oven to 350°F (175°C). Bake the buns for 15–18 minutes, until golden.

Vegan roti John

*Use gluten-free
bread.*

Serves 2

—

Prep time: 15 minutes
Cooking time: 20 minutes

two 6-inch (15 cm) baguettes
   (or 2 hot dog buns)
oil or vegan butter, for
   toasting the bread
sriracha or Sambal (page
   121), vegan mayonnaise and
   cucumber slices, to serve

"Ground beef"
1 teaspoon vegetable oil
1 red onion, finely chopped
2 garlic cloves, finely chopped
½ cup (40 g) TVP granules,
   prepared (page 25)
2 teaspoons curry powder
2 teaspoons ground cumin
¼ teaspoon salt

"Omelet"
half 12-ounce (340 g) block
   silken tofu
¼ cup (60 ml) plant milk
¼ cup (30 g) chickpea flour
¼ teaspoon salt
pinch of ground turmeric
1 teaspoon cornstarch
pinch of baking powder
black salt, for sprinkling

Like all good dishes, roti John has a great story behind it. According to local legend, when a hawker in Singapore was asked for a hamburger he made the inspired decision to pile egg and meat into a baguette lavishly spread with butter. He named his creation roti John, or "John's bread," after the puzzled tourist he first served it to. And it truly is an odd concoction, this Singaporean hamburger, with its crisp, eggy filling nestled in soft bread. It also goes well with some Sambal, if you feel so inclined.

First make the "ground beef." Heat the oil in a nonstick frying pan over medium heat, then fry the onion and garlic until fragrant and soft, about 3 minutes. Add the TVP and spices and continue to fry until the spices are aromatic and the TVP looks fluffy and less wet. Season with salt, then transfer to a bowl.

Slice each baguette in half lengthwise, but without cutting it through completely, so you can open it like a book. Spread a thin layer of oil or vegan butter on the inside and toast them in the hot frying pan, then set aside.

For the "omelet," put all the ingredients in a blender or food processor and blend to a smooth batter, then stir in the fried TVP mixture.

Set the frying pan over medium heat, greasing it lightly if necessary, then pour in half of the batter. Let the mixture cook, using a spatula to shape it into a rectangle roughly the size of the split-open baguette. Cook until the bottom is set but the top is still runny, about 3 minutes. Place a toasted baguette, split-side down, on top of the omelet. Use a spatula to tuck in any bits of omelet peeking out from under the baguette, then cover the pan and cook for a further 3–5 minutes.

When the omelet is completely set, carefully flip it and the baguette over and turn out onto a plate. Drizzle some sriracha or Sambal onto the omelet, and add a dab of vegan mayo if you like. Tuck in some slices of fresh cucumber, then fold the baguette closed. Repeat with the remaining omelet mixture and the second baguette.

Glutinous rice peanut balls

Serves 2

—

Prep time: 15 minutes
Cooking time: 15 minutes

Shallot oil
½ cup (125 ml) vegetable oil
5 shallots, finely sliced

¾ cup (100 g) glutinous rice
   flour
½ cup (110 g) white sugar
½ cup (70 g) ground roasted
   peanuts

It would be difficult to overstate the ubiquity of peanuts in Singaporean cooking. And these sweet, peanut-coated rice balls called *muah chee* are no exception. They were a recess-time favorite of mine at school – no day was complete without a plastic tub crammed full of *muah chee*. Use a toothpick to skewer them, then eat and let it soothe your rumbling stomach. Pure, peanutty bliss.

For the shallot oil, heat the oil in a saucepan or wok and fry the shallots until golden and crisp. Remove from the heat, letting the shallots infuse the oil until it is cool, then strain into a sterilized glass jar. (You only need a tablespoon plus 1 teaspoon of the shallot oil for this, but the rest should keep in a cool, dark place for 3–4 months and can be used to add extra flavor to stir-fries and curries.)

Set a steamer basket over a saucepan of boiling water. In a heatproof bowl that will fit inside your steamer basket, mix the rice flour, and ¼ cup (55 g) of the sugar with 1 tablespoon plus 1 teaspoon of your shallot oil and ¾ cup (185 ml) water to make a smooth, lump-free batter. Place the bowl of batter in the steamer basket and steam for 15 minutes, stirring halfway through with a spatula.

Meanwhile, mix together the peanuts and the rest of the sugar in a wide, shallow bowl.

When the dough is ready, transfer it into the peanut mixture. Holding a pair of scissors in one hand and a spoon in the other, cut the dough into small balls, and use the spoon to toss them about and coat them in the peanut mixture – this will also help to keep them from sticking together.

For easy eating, serve with toothpicks!

NOTE To make these in the microwave, cook the batter on high (in a microwave-safe bowl covered with plastic wrap) for 1 minute, then stir, cover and cook for another minute. Stir one more time and microwave for a final 30 seconds.

NUT-FREE Use black sesame seeds instead of peanuts.

Pandan and coconut dumplings

 GF

Makes 20 – enough for 4
—
Prep time: 20 minutes
Cooking time: 40 minutes

Dough
½ cup (85 g) small sweet
    potato cubes
⅔ cup (85 g) glutinous rice
    flour
pinch of salt

Coconut mixture
½ cup (40 g) freshly grated
    coconut or ½ cup (35 g)
    dried shredded coconut
1 pandan leaf, cut into short
    strips
¼ teaspoon salt
2.5 ounces (70 g) palm sugar,
    or ⅓ cup (70 g) coconut
    sugar or dark brown sugar

These dumplings, called *onde onde*, were one of the first things I learned to make in home economics classes at school. They are little dumplings that pop like a water balloon when you bite into them and ooze a delightfully floral caramel goo. When rolling these, take care not to roll the skin too thin or the dumplings might burst in the pan as they cook, rather than as you chew them. For this recipe, try to get the type of palm sugar that comes in a block, as it is easier to work with.

Steam the sweet potato until tender and easily pierced with a fork, about 5–7 minutes. Transfer to a bowl and add the flour, salt and 2½ tablespoons cold water. Mash with a potato masher until you have a smooth, thick dough. Chill in the refrigerator while you prepare the rest of the ingredients.

Put the grated coconut, pandan leaf and salt in a bowl or cake pan that will fit inside your steamer basket. Mix well, then steam over a pan of boiling water for 15–20 minutes, until fragrant and the coconut is soft.

If you are using palm sugar in block form, cut it into small chunks or cubes, as this makes it easier to stuff into the dumplings. If you are using a granulated sugar, like coconut sugar or dark brown sugar, it will be slightly trickier to stuff the dumplings, but not impossible!

Bring a large saucepan of water to a boil. Divide the dough into twenty balls. Flatten a ball in the palm of your hand and press a cube of sugar (or ½–1 teaspoon granulated sugar) into the middle of the dough, then close up the dough and form it back into a ball, encasing the sugar in the middle. Make sure there are no holes in the dough, or the sugar will ooze out as the dumpling cooks. Immediately drop the dumpling into the boiling water and make the next dumplings. Stop making the dumplings if the pan becomes overcrowded at any stage, and just wait until some of them have finished cooking.

The dumplings are done when they float to the surface, about 3–5 minutes. Use a slotted spoon to scoop them out, then drop into the steamed coconut and toss to coat.

These dumplings are best served warm, while the sugar is still molten – but let them cool for 5 minutes before diving in, so you don't burn your mouth.

Almond and semolina sugee cake

Serves 12

—

Prep time: 30 minutes (plus overnight softening time)
Cooking time: 45 minutes

½ cup (115 g) vegan butter
1½ cups (300 g) fine
  semolina
1 cup (250 ml) plant milk
½ cup (75 g) all-purpose flour
1 cup (130 g) firmly packed
  confectioners' sugar
½ cup (130 g) vegan yogurt or
  ½ cup (125 ml) coconut milk
1 teaspoon baking powder
½ teaspoon baking soda
pinch of salt
½ teaspoon vanilla extract
½ teaspoon almond extract
1 tablespoon plus 1 teaspoon
  agave syrup
1 tablespoon plus 1 teaspoon
  brandy
½ teaspoon ground cinnamon
¼ cup (40 g) finely chopped
  almonds

Vegan marzipan
1½ cups (150 g) almond meal
1 cup (110 g) sifted
  confectioners' sugar
1 tablespoon plus 1 teaspoon
  maple syrup
1 teaspoon lemon juice
¼ teaspoon almond extract –
  optional

2½ tablespoons apricot jam,
  for brushing
flaked almonds and whole
  pistachios, to garnish

Sugee cake and I have history: We go way back. Every birthday, wedding or celebration culminated in the slicing of one of these gloriously golden cakes. No one made this cake quite like my grandpa did – he was something of an expert, despite never following a formal recipe himself. This cake is usually laden with egg yolk (at least six) and butter, to be eaten in small slices. As you can imagine, it wasn't the easiest thing to make vegan, but I kept at it until I cracked it. I figured I owed it to myself, as I never did get that eighteenth-birthday sugee cake. . . .

Cream the vegan butter in a large bowl to soften it, then mix in the semolina and plant milk. Cover the bowl and chill in the fridge overnight to soften the semolina.

Next day, preheat the oven to 350°F (180°C), and grease and line a 7-inch (18 cm) round cake pan. Take the bowl of semolina from the fridge and sift in the flour and sugar. Stir well, then add the yogurt, baking powder, baking soda, salt, vanilla and almond extracts, agave syrup, brandy and cinnamon. Mix until just combined, then fold in the almonds. Pour the batter into the pan and bake for 45 minutes, or until a skewer inserted in the center comes out clean.

Meanwhile, make the marzipan. In a food processor, blitz the ground almonds for 30–60 seconds to make them a little finer – but don't over process or you'll end up with almond butter! Transfer to a large bowl and sift in the icing sugar. Drizzle in the maple syrup, lemon juice, 1 tablespoon plus 1 teaspoon water, and the almond extract, if using. Knead until it starts to come together. Shape into a ball, then flatten into a disc – this will make it easier to roll it out later. Wrap in plastic wrap and chill for at least an hour before using.

Let the cake cool completely before turning out of the pan. Roll out the marzipan into a 7-inch (18 cm) circle. Warm the apricot jam in a small pan (or the microwave) and brush over the top of the cake. Lay the marzipan onto the cake, then garnish with almonds and pistachios.

NOTE This cake is not too sweet, even with the apricot jam and marzipan, so it's perfect for anyone without much of a sweet tooth. However, if you like your cakes a bit sweeter, add up to ¼ cup (30 g) more confectioners' sugar and another tablespoon plus 1 teaspoon of plant milk.

Pandan waffles with coconut peanut butter

Serves 4–6

Prep time: 20 minutes
Cooking time: 25 minutes

2½ tablespoons aquafaba
  (page 11)
1 cup (250 ml) coconut milk
¼ cup (60 ml) melted
  coconut oil
¼ cup (55 g) white sugar
1 cup (150 g) all-purpose
  flour, sifted
1 tablespoon plus 1 teaspoon
  cornstarch
2 teaspoons baking powder
pinch of salt
½ teaspoon pandan extract
  (or 1 teaspoon vanilla or
  coconut extract, plus a
  few drops of green food
  coloring)

Coconut peanut butter
1½ cups (200 g) roasted
  peanuts
¼ cup (25 g) desiccated
  coconut
¼–½ teaspoon salt
1 tablespoon plus 1 teaspoon
  maple syrup

coconut flakes, to garnish

These were the ultimate treat growing up. My father would often arrive home, a rumpled white paper bag stained with telltale splotches of peanut oil in hand. And if that wasn't enough of a clue, the smell would hit you soon after: pandan, peanuts and the vanilla-sweet whiff of coconut. The waffles themselves are a vivid shade of green, and when eaten warm (as they should be), their crevices harbor little reservoirs of molten, oozing peanut butter. If you do not have a high-speed blender, you can slather the waffles with whatever peanut butter you have on hand. While you will need a waffle iron to make the batter into waffles, don't worry if you don't have one: You can just fry the batter in a hot nonstick frying pan to make pancakes, or, even better, on a ridged grill pan, so you'll still get crevices where the peanut butter can pool.

Preheat your waffle iron. Whisk the aquafaba until frothy, then add the coconut milk, coconut oil, sugar, flour, cornstarch, baking powder, salt, and pandan extract, and mix just until everything comes together – be careful not to overmix the batter.

Once the waffle iron is hot and ready, ladle ½ cup (125 ml) batter into each waffle-well and close the lid. Let it cook until it beeps, then remove it. Keep going until all the batter is used up.

Meanwhile, for the coconut peanut butter, blend the peanuts, coconut and salt in a high-speed blender until creamy. If you have a less powerful blender, you'll probably need to add a few teaspoons of a neutral-flavored oil to help it along. Add the syrup and stir well. Because you have just blended it, the coconut peanut butter should be slightly warm – perfect for serving!

When all your waffles are cooked, serve with a good dollop of peanut butter and garnish with coconut flakes.

Coconut kaya custard

 GF

Prep time: 20 minutes
Cook time: 40 minutes

1½ cups (250 g) winter
squash or sweet potato
cubes
½ cup (125 ml) coconut milk
2 pandan leaves, knotted, or
½ teaspoon pandan extract
(or vanilla extract)
¼ cup (50 g) grated palm
sugar (or dark brown sugar)

While this is officially a breakfast staple, you will happen upon many a *kopitiam* (coffee shop) where locals sit throughout the day, nursing their kopi (coffee) with a side of kaya toast. This coconut custard is often slathered onto thick slabs of bread, along with a generous wedge of salted butter – although I also find it delightful smeared on crackers or rippled through some piping-hot porridge.

Boil, steam or microwave the squash until soft. Transfer it into a food processor, along with the coconut milk, and process until very smooth.

Transfer to a saucepan and add the pandan leaves or extract and the sugar. Bring to a boil, stirring occasionally, then lower the heat and let it simmer until thickened, about 20–30 minutes. Remove the pandan leaves and let the custard cool, then store in a clean jar in the fridge for up to a week.

Mung bean porridge

Serves 4

—

**Prep time: 20 minutes
(plus soaking time)
Cooking time: 35 minutes**

2 inches (5 cm) ginger
1 cup (225 g) green mung
    beans, soaked overnight
    and drained
½ cup (110 g) white sugar
½ teaspoon salt
1 pandan leaf, knotted, or 1
    teaspoon pandan extract
1 cup (250 ml) coconut milk

Beans commonly feature in Asian desserts. The Japanese cook adzuki beans until they collapse into a silky paste, and the Chinese use them to thicken soy milk into a wobbly custard. In Malaysia, green mung beans are stewed down in an aromatic broth, which is then augmented with coconut milk. The resulting porridge, *bubur kacang hijau*, is ambrosial – comforting and decadent.

Using a pair of tongs, hold the ginger over a low flame until charred. If you don't have a gas stove, you can skip this step, but it does give the ginger a more mellow, complex flavor.

Place the ginger, mung beans, sugar, salt, pandan and 4 cups (1 liter) water in a saucepan. Bring to a boil, then reduce the heat and simmer until the beans are soft and tender, about 30 minutes.

Stir in the coconut milk and bring back up to a simmer, then take it off the heat and serve. The porridge can also be kept in the fridge for 2–3 days and eaten cold.

Cendol

 GF

Serves 4
—
Prep time: 30 minutes
Cooking time: 20 minutes

Pandan syrup
½ cup (100 g) lightly packed grated palm sugar or brown sugar
1 pandan leaf, knotted

Pandan jelly
⅓ cup (55 g) rice flour
2 tablespoons tapioca starch
2 teaspoons pandan extract
¼ teaspoon salt
ice cubes

1 cup (125 ml) crushed ice – optional
¾ cup (95 g) cooked adzuki beans – optional
one 13.5 ounce (400 ml) can coconut milk

This colorful drink is traditionally made with coconut milk, red adzuki beans and emerald, jellylike noodles. Luminescent and unsettlingly wormlike, the jelly noodles can be a bit hard to wrap your head around – but trust me, *cendol* just isn't quite the same without them. You will need a cheese grater with large holes, which you can use to squeeze the jelly through and create the little strands. Otherwise, a slotted spoon with circular holes or something similar will do the trick.

Cendol is generally served over shaved ice or very cold: oh-so-inviting in the tropical heat of Singapore, but equally enticing even if it's cold and rainy in your corner of the world.

Put the sugar and pandan leaf in a small saucepan with ¼ cup (60 ml) water. Bring to a boil, then let it simmer for 15–20 minutes, until the sugar has dissolved to form a dark, caramel-like syrup. Leave to cool.

Meanwhile, make the pandan jelly. Put the rice flour, tapioca starch, pandan extract, salt and 1½ cups (375 ml) water in a saucepan and whisk until smooth and lump-free. Have ready a large bowl of iced water. Place the jelly mixture over medium heat and cook, stirring constantly, until it thickens and forms a very thick, glossy paste, about 5–7 minutes. Remove from the heat and, holding a cheese grater with coarse holes over the bowl of iced water, drop a large dollop of jelly mixture onto the grater, then use a large spoon to press the jelly through the holes into the ice-cold water. Repeat until all the jelly is used up. Leave the jelly strands in the water for 15 minutes before gently draining and placing in a bowl. Set aside until ready to serve.

To serve, place some crushed ice, if using, in each glass. Add some adzuki beans, if using, then a scoop of pandan jelly. Pour in some coconut milk – the amount you use will depend on how creamy you like your cendol. Drizzle with a thin layer of syrup and serve right away.

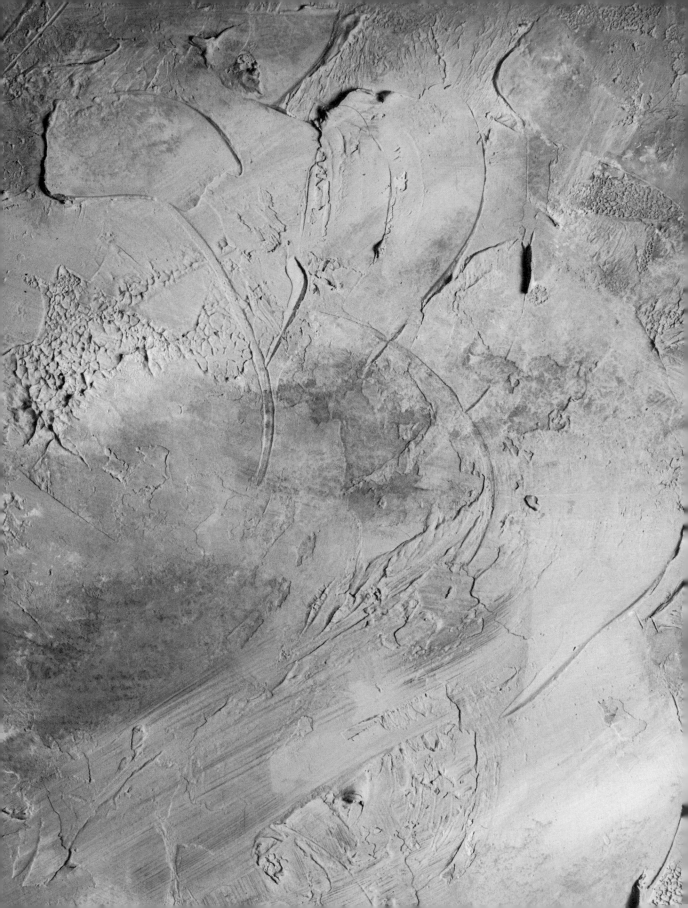

04
China

The West has been infatuated with Chinese cuisine for decades. Stir-fry sauces line our supermarket shelves and dim sum restaurants are packed with foodies who have mastered the art of eating with chopsticks – to a degree, at least!

But many of the dishes we know and love bear only a passing resemblance to the food served in China itself. Authentic Chinese cuisine is steeped in tradition. In a country with such a rich and extensive history, eight different regional cuisines rise above the rest. These are known as "the eight cuisines" and they owe their differences to the geographic variations across China. Food eaten in villages hidden among the peaks of misty mountains is vastly different to that enjoyed in cities surrounded by lush forest. Similarly, the different ethnic groups and cultures have their own food cultures as well. Light and perfumed Cantonese cuisine is perhaps the most popular of the eight and is what most of us associate with Chinese food from takeout or in dim sum restaurants. Sichuan food, bold and feisty, is also renowned, laced with fiery chilies and mouth-numbing Sichuan peppercorns.

You may be no stranger to some sweet and sour, followed by a fortune cookie or two. But, as you slurp on soup dumplings and bite through the flaky, buttery crust of a custard tart, you will realize that nothing comes close to proper Chinese food.

Rice noodle rolls

Use a gluten-free hoisin sauce.

Makes 8 rolls
(enough for 4 as a snack)
—
Prep time: 30 minutes
Cooking time: 1 hour

1 cup (160 g) rice flour
2 tablespoons cornstarch
1 tablespoon tapioca starch
1 tablespoon vegetable oil,
    plus extra for greasing
2 scallions, finely sliced, plus
    extra to garnish
2½ tablespoons sesame
    seeds, plus extra to garnish
crispy fried shallots, for
    sprinkling – optional

Dipping sauce
½ cup (125 ml) hoisin sauce
¼ cup (60 ml) boiling water

There is a place near my house that makes absolutely amazing *chee chong fun*: supple, slippery rice noodles flecked with slivers of scallion. I like to drown mine in sweet, tangy hoisin sauce – but for something lighter, you can dip the rolls in briny soy sauce.

Set a steamer basket over a pan of boiling water. Place a square pan inside the steamer – I like to use an 8-inch (20 cm) square brownie pan but if your basket is too small to hold a pan of this size, any metal baking pan with a flat base should work. Let the pan heat up in the steamer for about 15 minutes.

Meanwhile, prepare the batter by whisking together the flour, cornstarch, tapioca starch and oil with 1¾ cups (435 ml) water until smooth and lump-free.

Carefully lift out the hot pan from the steamer and brush it with a thin layer of oil. Return it to the steamer basket for 5 minutes, then scoop a ladleful of the batter into the pan, to form a thin layer on the base. Sprinkle with a few slices of scallion and sesame seeds, then cover and steam for 5 minutes until set.

When the batter is cooked, use a dough scraper to loosen the cooked batter from one edge of the pan. Continue to loosen it, rolling it up as you go along. Remove the completed noodle roll from the pan and brush with another thin layer of oil, then return to the steamer for 5 minutes to heat through. Repeat until all the batter has been cooked. If needed, return all the rolls to the steamer for 1–2 minutes to warm through before serving.

For the dipping sauce, simply mix the hoisin sauce and hot water together in a small bowl until smooth.

Serve the rolls with the sauce on the side for dipping, or drizzle it on top. Garnish with more scallion slices and sesame seeds, and sprinkle with some crispy fried shallots, if you like.

Brown rice congee with stewed peanuts

Use tamari instead of dark soy sauce.

Serves 4

—

Prep time: 20 minutes
Cooking time: 2 hours

Stewed peanuts
1 cup (140 g) raw peanuts
½ teaspoon ground cinnamon
½ teaspoon five spice powder
2½ tablespoons dark soy sauce
1 tablespoon plus 1 teaspoon brown sugar
3 garlic cloves, crushed

1 cup (200 g) brown rice
½ cup (100 g) red split lentils
10 cups (2½ liters) vegetable stock
3 dried shiitake mushrooms – optional
2 inches (5 cm) ginger, finely chopped
4 garlic cloves, finely chopped
½ teaspoon salt
sesame oil, sliced scallions, crispy fried shallots and soy sauce, to garnish

Congee is to Asians what chicken soup is to Westerners. We have it when we are ill, or cold, or sad. When I was growing up, I would seek solace in a deep bowl of congee whenever I got my braces tightened. There is something profoundly comforting about it, despite its simplicity. Although it takes a long time to cook, once it is in the pot congee pretty much takes care of itself.

First make the stewed peanuts. Put all the ingredients in a small saucepan with 2 cups (500 ml) water and stir well. Simmer over low heat for about 2 hours, until the peanuts are incredibly tender and soft. Keep an eye on it to make sure it doesn't boil dry – add a splash more water if needed.

In a large saucepan, mix together all the remaining ingredients except the garnishes, then bring to a boil over medium heat. Turn down to a simmer, cover and leave to cook until the rice and lentils have softened and almost disintegrated, releasing their starch and thickening the liquid. This should take 1–1½ hours, depending on how thick you like your congee. Give it a stir every so often and add a little water if it seems to be getting too thick.

To serve, ladle some congee into each bowl. Top with a generous helping of stewed peanuts, and garnish liberally with sesame oil, scallions, fried shallots and soy sauce.

How to fold the dumplings

Place a spoonful of filling on the wrapper and wet the edge with water, using your finger.

Fold the bottom half of the wrapper up, over the filling.

Press to seal the edges together, trying not to get any air trapped around the filling.

Start to crimp the edge of the jiaozi.

Continue to crimp the jiaozi, about 5-7 times.

Mushroom and chive dumplings

GF

Buy gluten-free dumpling skins, and use tamari in place of the soy sauce.

Makes 30 (enough for 4–6)
—
Prep time: 30 minutes
Cooking time: 20 minutes

Filling
1 cup (100 g) very finely chopped mushrooms
1 cup (80 g) finely chopped scallions
½ cup (80 g) grated carrot
1 cup (75 g) finely chopped napa cabbage or savoy cabbage
½ cup (80 g) cooked rice vermicelli noodles, roughly chopped into shorter lengths
2 teaspoons light soy sauce
1 tablespoon plus 1 teaspoon cornstarch
2 teaspoons sesame oil

30 store-bought or homemade dumpling skins (page 21)
1 tablespoon plus 1 teaspoon vegetable oil and 1 teaspoon sesame oil, if frying the dumplings
light soy sauce, to serve

Whenever I go to my favorite dim sum restaurant back home in Singapore, *jiaozi* are always the first thing I order. These are often steamed, but I find that frying them first, letting their bases caramelize, gives the finished dumplings a satisfying crunch. You should be able to find vermicelli rice noodles, or thin rice noodles, in any supermarket, often in the Asian food aisle or the noodle section. If you have the dried sort, just boil the noodles for 3 minutes, then dunk immediately into a bowl of cold water and drain well.

Put all the filling ingredients into a large bowl and mix well with your hands to make sure everything is thoroughly coated and evenly distributed.

Fill and fold the dumplings as shown opposite. Repeat until you have used up all the filling and dumpling skins.

To steam the dumplings, line a steamer basket with parchment paper and fit in as many dumplings, seam side up, as you can without overcrowding – you need to leave gaps between them. Set the steamer basket over a pan of boiling water and steam the dumplings for 10–12 minutes, then repeat for the remaining dumplings.

To fry the dumplings, set a skillet over medium-high heat and add the vegetable oil. Fill the pan with dumplings, seam side up, and fry until their bottoms are golden and crisp, about 3 minutes. Add enough water to the pan to half-submerge the dumplings, then immediately cover the pan and let the dumplings steam for 3 minutes. Uncover the pan, drizzle the dumplings with the sesame oil and keep cooking until all the water has evaporated.

Serve the dumplings warm with a small bowl of light soy sauce for dipping.

Scallion pancakes

Makes 8 pancakes

—

Prep time: 20 minutes
Cooking time: 10 minutes

½ cup (125 ml) vegetable
   stock
¼ teaspoon salt
½ teaspoon garlic powder –
   optional
1¼ cups (185 g) all-purpose
   flour, plus extra for dusting

Dipping sauce
1 tablespoon plus 1 teaspoon
   light soy sauce
1 teaspoon Chinese black
   vinegar or rice vinegar
1 teaspoon mirin
1 teaspoon sesame oil
1 scallion, sliced
½ teaspoon sriracha
1 teaspoon sugar

2½ tablespoons sesame oil,
   for brushing
2 scallions, finely chopped
vegetable oil, for frying

The perfect marriage of chewy and flaky, this popular Chinese appetizer is a breeze to make at home. When frying the pancakes, use at least a teaspoon of oil for each one – this ensures they get scorched and golden in patches, otherwise they'll be all chew and no flake!

Bring the vegetable stock to a boil, then add the salt and garlic powder and stir to dissolve. Sift the flour into a large heatproof bowl, then slowly pour in the hot stock. Stir with a wooden spoon until the dough starts to come together, then transfer onto a flour-dusted work surface. Let it cool slightly if it is still too hot to handle and then knead until you have a smooth, elastic ball of dough – this should take about 5 minutes. Put the dough into a clean bowl, cover with plastic wrap and leave to rest for at least 30 minutes.

Meanwhile, make the dipping sauce by mixing all the ingredients together.

Put the sesame oil in a shallow bowl. Roll the rested dough into a log and divide into eight. Take one dough portion and roll it out with a rolling pin into a circle about 3 mm thick. Lightly brush with sesame oil, then sprinkle with about a teaspoon of scallion. Starting from one edge, roll the dough up into a tight roll, as if you were making cinnamon buns. Pinch the ends of the roll to seal, then coil up the roll of dough like a snail shell. Now use your rolling pin to roll it out again into a thin pancake. It is this coiling and rolling that creates the flaky layers in your pancake. Repeat for all the other dough balls.

When you're ready to cook your pancakes, pour a little vegetable oil into a nonstick frying pan over medium heat. Fry each pancake for about 1 minute on each side, or until lightly golden with spots of brown.

Serve the pancakes with a bowl of the dipping sauce.

Sweet and sour mushrooms

 Use rice flour instead of all-purpose, and use gluten-free bread crumbs.

Serves 2

—

Prep time: 25 minutes
Cooking time: 30 minutes

¼ cup (35 g) bread crumbs
¼ teaspoon salt
¼ cup (35 g) all-purpose flour
¼ teaspoon chili powder
¼ teaspoon white pepper
¼ cup (60 ml) plant milk
10 button mushrooms

Sweet and sour sauce

1 tablespoon plus 1 teaspoon
    vegetable oil
1 red onion, roughly sliced
1 small red bell pepper,
    seeded and sliced
1 small green bell pepper,
    seeded and sliced
1 celery stalk, sliced
1 cup (160 g) pineapple
    chunks
½ cup (125 ml) pineapple
    juice
1 teaspoon sugar
pinch of salt
2½ tablespoons lemon juice
¼ cup (60 g) ketchup
1 tablespoon plus 1 teaspoon
    sriracha – optional

sliced scallion and sesame
    seeds, to garnish
steamed rice, to serve

Mushrooms can be polarizing: I know some people who love them and others who can't stand them. If you happen to belong to the latter group, feel free to swap the mushrooms for another vegetable, such as cauliflower, or even tofu – just remember to adjust the baking time. And if you plan on serving this sometime after cooking it, keep the mushrooms separate until you're ready to eat, as their crispy battered exterior will soften if they're left sitting in the sauce for too long.

Preheat the oven to 400°F (200°C).

Lightly toast the bread crumbs in a dry frying pan until golden. Lay out three shallow bowls on your countertop: In the first, toss together the toasted bread crumbs and half of the salt. In the second bowl, mix the flour, chili powder, pepper and the rest of the salt, then pour the plant milk into the last bowl. Line a baking sheet with parchment paper or a silicone mat. Take a mushroom and toss it in the flour mix until well coated. Now dip it quickly into the milk so the flour goes tacky, then quickly transfer it to the bread crumbs, toss to coat well and place it on the baking sheet. Coat the rest of the mushrooms in the same way, then bake for 12–15 minutes, until golden and crispy.

Meanwhile, make the sweet and sour sauce. Pour the oil in a large nonstick frying pan over medium heat and fry the onion until translucent, soft and fragrant, about 5 minutes. Add the bell peppers, celery and ½ cup (125 ml) water, then cover and cook until the peppers are soft and the celery has lost its bite, about 5–7 minutes. Now add the pineapple chunks and juice, sugar, salt, lemon juice, ketchup and sriracha, if using. Let the sauce cook, uncovered, for 5–7 minutes, stirring occasionally.

Add the crispy baked mushrooms to the sweet and sour sauce and stir well to coat. Garnish with scallion and sesame seeds, then serve immediately, with steamed rice.

Peddler's noodles

GF

Use tamari in place of soy sauce, and rice or buckwheat noodles instead of wheat.

Depending on how much chili oil you use.

Serves 4

—

Prep time: 30 minutes
Cooking time: 25 minutes

"Ground pork"
2 teaspoons vegetable oil
4 garlic cloves, finely chopped
1 cm ginger, finely chopped
1 shallot, very finely chopped
2 scallions, chopped
1 tablespoon plus 1 teaspoon
   dark soy sauce
1 cup (80 g) TVP granules,
   prepared (page 25)
pinch of white pepper

4 nests (7 ounces/200 g)
   dried wheat noodles

Sauce
1 teaspoon sesame oil
2½ tablespoons tahini
2 teaspoons peanut butter –
   optional
½ teaspoon white sugar
1 tablespoon plus 1 teaspoon
   light soy sauce
2–4 teaspoons Chili oil
   (page 20)

2 cups (500 ml) hot
   vegetable stock
sliced scallion, sesame seeds
   and chili oil, to serve

Dan dan mian, or peddler's noodles, are a favorite in my family, and in many Chinese restaurants. There are many versions of these noodles, but in my opinion the best one is soupy, enriched with buttery sesame paste and speckled with amber flecks of chili oil. I like to perk mine up with a dollop of peanut butter, which is not traditional but lends the broth a marvelous nutty undertone. Eat piping hot . . . and slurping is mandatory.

First, prepare the "ground pork." Pour the oil into a wok or frying pan over medium heat and fry the garlic, ginger and shallot until fragrant, about 3 minutes, then add the scallions and dark soy sauce. Fry for 2 minutes before adding the drained TVP and pepper, then continue frying for another 3–4 minutes so the TVP is heated through and starting to look dry and fluffy. Cover and set aside.

Cook the noodles according to the package instructions. For the sauce, whisk the sesame oil, tahini, peanut butter, if using, sugar, light soy sauce, chili oil and 1 tablespoon plus 1 teaspoon water into a smooth paste. Divide between four bowls.

Drain the noodles and divide between the bowls. Toss the noodles in the sauce, then pour ½ cup (125 ml) hot stock into each bowl. Add a large spoonful of the TVP mixture, then garnish with sliced scallion, sesame seeds and more chili oil, if desired.

Gua bao with sweet potato "belly"

 GF

Use tamari in place of soy sauce, and double-check to make sure the vinegar is gluten-free.

Serves 4

—

Prep time: 30 minutes
Cooking time: 1 hour

¾ cup (185 ml) lukewarm water
2½ tablespoons white sugar
2 teaspoons active dry yeast
2 cups (300 g) all-purpose flour, plus extra for dusting
¼ teaspoon salt
½ teaspoon baking powder
1 tablespoon plus 1 teaspoon vegetable oil

Sweet potato "belly"
3 sweet potatoes, peeled
6 garlic cloves, crushed
four 1-inch (2.5 cm) pieces ginger
4 star anise
pinch of white pepper
¼ teaspoon five spice powder
2 tablespoons rice wine or dry white wine
¼ cup (60 ml) light soy sauce
1 teaspoon white sugar

Pickle
1 small cucumber
1 small carrot
½ teaspoon sesame oil
2½ tablespoons rice vinegar or apple cider vinegar
1 teaspoon white sugar
1 teaspoon light soy sauce

Crushed peanuts, cilantro and sriracha sauce, to serve

Originally from Taiwan, *gua bao* is a popular street food whose fame has spread rapidly, thanks in part to Momofuku. Here's my spin on it: a balancing act of succulent sweet potato "belly," briny pickle and crunchy peanuts.

First make the bun dough. In a large bowl, combine the water, sugar and yeast and set aside until frothy, about 5 minutes. Sift in the flour, then add the salt, baking powder and oil. Knead until the dough comes together, then transfer onto a countertop and knead for about 7 minutes, until it forms a smooth elastic ball. Return the dough to the bowl, cover with a damp kitchen towel and leave in a warm place to rise for about 1 hour, until it has doubled in size.

Meanwhile, prepare the sweet potato "belly." Slice each sweet potato lengthwise into four, then cut each slice in half lengthwise, giving you eight flat wedges from each sweet potato. Put them in a large saucepan with the other ingredients and ¼ cup (60 ml) water, then cover and cook over low heat for about 30 minutes, until very tender.

For the pickle, use a vegetable peeler to cut the cucumber and carrot into ribbons. Place in a bowl with the rest of the ingredients. Toss well, then chill until you are ready to eat.

When the bun dough has risen, knock it back with your fist, then transfer onto a well-floured countertop. Divide into eight equal portions, then roll out each one into an oval about 5 x 3 inches (13 x 7.5 cm). Now you can either brush half of the oval with oil, or cut a square of parchment paper to lay over half of it. Fold over the other half – the oil or paper should keep it from sticking. When all the buns are shaped, leave in a warm place, covered, for 20 minutes.

Line the base of your steamer basket with parchment paper and set it over a pan of boiling water. Pop three or four buns into the steamer basket, spacing them well apart. Cover, lower the heat so the water is just simmering and steam for 15 minutes, or until springy. Briefly lift the lid every 5 minutes to let the heat escape, or the dough will rise too quickly and then collapse, giving you wrinkly buns.

To assemble your gua bao, fill a bun with a few wedges of sweet potato, some pickle, a sprinkle of peanuts and cilantro, and a drizzle of sriracha. For extra flavor, dip the gua bao in a little of the sweet potato broth as you eat.

China

Mapo tofu

Serves 4

—

Prep time: 20 minutes
Cooking time: 20 minutes

1 tablespoon plus 1 teaspoon
vegetable oil
2 garlic cloves, finely chopped
1 inch (2.5 cm) ginger, finely
chopped
½ cup (40 g) TVP granules,
prepared (page 25)
1 tablespoon plus 1 teaspoon
miso paste
1 tablespoon plus 1 teaspoon
doubanjiang (chili bean
sauce)
1 cup (250 ml) vegetable
stock
1 tablespoon plus 1 teaspoon
dark soy sauce
one 14-ounce (400 g) block
extra-firm tofu, pressed
(page 25) and cubed
½ teaspoon cornstarch
1 teaspoon sesame oil
½ teaspoon white sugar
sliced scallion, red chili and
sesame seeds, to garnish
steamed rice, to serve

This dish calls for a Chinese fermented fava bean paste known as *doubanjiang*, which can usually be found in larger supermarkets or local Asian shops. If you have no luck, simply substitute with 1 more tablespoon plus 1 teaspoon of miso and 1 teaspoon of sriracha – the flavor will be slightly different, but still wickedly tasty. I like to use firm tofu here, as it holds up well to stir-frying, but if you are gentle, silken tofu also works well and is much more traditional.

Heat the oil in a large nonstick frying pan over medium heat and fry the garlic and ginger for 1–2 minutes, until fragrant. Add the drained TVP and fry for another minute or so. Next, stir in the miso and doubanjiang until no large clumps remain – add a splash of the stock to help dissolve the pastes, if necessary. Once it's smooth, pour in the rest of the stock and the soy sauce. Stir well, then bring to a boil and add the tofu to the pan.

In a small bowl, whisk the cornstarch with 1 tablespoon plus 1 teaspoon water until smooth. Pour into the pan, stirring as you do so, to prevent lumps from forming. Cook, stirring constantly, until the liquid starts to thicken, about 3–5 minutes.

Add the sesame oil and sugar, mix and take the pan off the heat. Garnish with the sliced scallion and chili, sprinkle with sesame seeds, then serve with steamed rice.

Shanghai soup dumplings

Makes 24–30 dumplings
(enough for 4–6)
—
Prep time: 20 minutes, plus
setting time
Cooking time: 20 minutes

Jellied stock
1½ cups (375 ml) vegetable
   stock
½ teaspoon agar powder

Filling
½ cup (40 g) TVP granules,
   prepared (page 25)
2 scallions, very finely
   chopped
1 teaspoon white sugar
1 tablespoon plus 1 teaspoon
   light soy sauce
¼ teaspoon sesame oil
pinch of white pepper
1 inch (2.5 cm) ginger, very
   finely chopped

1 quantity homemade
   Dumpling skins (page 21)*
black vinegar (or soy sauce)
   and slivers of ginger, for
   dipping

I have seen many a tourist fall victim to the piping-hot soup inside a *xiao long bao*. When eating these little dumplings, always cradle them in a soup spoon before biting into them and slurping up the molten stock. Trying to eat them using only chopsticks will almost definitely result in a hot-soup-in-your-lap situation. So cradle, bite, slurp. If the soup is still too hot after you bite into the dumpling, let it leak out into the spoon, where it can cool down ever so slightly.

First, make the jellied stock. Put the stock and agar into a small saucepan and bring to a boil, then lower the heat and simmer for 5 minutes. Pour into a heatproof bowl or plastic container and refrigerate until set, about 4–6 hours. I like to do this the day before.

To make the filling, combine the drained TVP, scallions, sugar, soy sauce, sesame oil, pepper and ginger in a bowl. Take the jellied stock out of the fridge and cut it into small cubes, then stir into the TVP mixture.

Line the base of a steamer basket with napa cabbage leaves or parchment paper and set it over a pan of boiling water. Take a dumpling skin and put it on the palm of your hand. Place a tablespoon of the TVP and jelly filling in the middle. Use the fingers of your free hand to wet the perimeter of the wrapper, then gather up the edges and pleat together at the top of the dumpling, pressing the wet edges together to seal.

Working in batches, place the dumplings in the steamer basket, leaving about 1 inch (2.5 cm) between them. Steam for 10 minutes, then serve warm, with a dipping sauce of black vinegar or soy sauce and slivers of ginger.

* I do not recommend using store-bought dumpling skins for soup dumplings, as they are too thin.

Lettuce cups

Serves 4 as a starter

—

Prep time: 15 minutes
Cooking time: 15 minutes

1 tablespoon plus 1 teaspoon
    vegetable oil
1 cup (80 g) TVP granules,
    prepared (page 25)
2 garlic cloves, finely chopped
1 cm ginger, finely chopped
2½ tablespoons vegetarian
    oyster sauce
2 teaspoons light soy sauce
1 tablespoon plus 1 teaspoon
    lime juice
one 8-ounce (227 g) can
    whole water chestnuts,
    drained and diced
2 scallions, sliced
1 teaspoon sesame oil
pinch of white pepper
1 head of butter lettuce
sliced red chili, scallion and
    crushed roasted peanuts,
    to serve

Another popular starter at Chinese restaurants, *san choy bao* is a joy to assemble and devour! The intense, savory filling piled inside the lettuce cups is studded with little chunks of water chestnut, which give a lovely crunch and a burst of freshness.

Heat the oil in a saucepan over medium heat. Add the drained TVP and cook until it starts to look dry and fluffy, about 3–5 minutes.

Stir in the garlic, ginger, oyster sauce, soy sauce, lime juice, water chestnuts, scallions, sesame oil and pepper. Continue to fry for 4–5 minutes, until the garlic and ginger have softened. Remove from the heat.

To serve, spoon several tablespoons of this mixture into the center of a lettuce leaf, scatter with chili, scallion and peanuts to taste, then roll up and eat taco-style.

How to fold the dumplings

Place a spoonful of filling in the middle of the wrapper.

Use your finger to wet the edge of the wrapper.

Fold the bottom half of the wrapper up, folding it in half.

Press to seal the edges together, pressing outward to remove any air around the filling.

Wet one side of the semicircle you formed.

Bring the edges together.

Press down firmly to attach them to each other.

Dumpling noodles

Makes 16 (enough for 4)

—

Prep time: 30 minutes
Cooking time: 30 minutes

Filling

½ cup (40 g) TVP granules
  (not soaked)
½ cup (125 ml) hot water
one 8-ounce (227 g) can
  water chestnuts, drained
  and very finely chopped
½ cup (50 g) very finely
  chopped chives
half 14-ounce (400 g) block
  extra-firm tofu, crumbled
1 inch (2.5 cm) ginger, very
  finely chopped
2 scallions, very finely
  chopped
2½ tablespoons light soy
  sauce
1 teaspoon sesame oil
1 teaspoon white sugar
½ teaspoon white pepper
2½ tablespoons cornstarch

16 store-bought or
  homemade dumpling skins
  (page 21)
4 nests (7 ounces/200 g)
  dried whole wheat noodles
2 large heads bok choy, cut in
  half lengthwise
¼ cup plus 1 tablespoon
  (75 g) ketchup
2 teaspoons dark soy sauce
2 teaspoons sesame oil

Back home in Singapore we were frequent patrons of a popular wonton noodle shop. My sister, Kyra, was smitten with dry wonton *mee*, where the dumplings and noodles are tossed in a viscous sauce. I preferred mine swimming in marbled, golden broth. This recipe is for the dry version, but feel free to ditch the sauce and swap it for some piping-hot vegetable stock.

Line a steamer basket with parchment paper and set it over a pan of boiling water.

For the filling, put the TVP in a heatproof bowl, pour in the hot water and leave to soak for 5 minutes. Add all the other filling ingredients and mix well.

Take a dumpling skin and place a tablespoon of the filling in the center, then fold as shown opposite. When all the dumplings are made, place them in your steamer basket, leaving about 1 inch (2.5 cm) between them, and steam for 15 minutes – you may need to do this in batches.

Meanwhile, cook the noodles according to the instructions on the package. Bring a small saucepan of water to a boil, add the bok choy and blanch for a minute, just until wilted, then drain.

Mix together the ketchup, soy sauce and sesame oil, then divide between four shallow serving bowls. Drain the noodles and divide between the bowls. Toss well to coat the noodles in the sauce – you may need to add a spoonful of the noodle-cooking water to loosen the sauce slightly. Add four steamed dumplings and some bok choy to each bowl, and get slurping!

NOTE To make the soup version of this dish, instead of tossing the noodles with the ketchup, soy sauce and sesame oil, just pour 1 cup (250 ml) hot vegetable stock over the drained noodles in each bowl.

"Egg drop" soup

 GF

Serves 4 as a side
—
Prep time: 15 minutes
Cooking time: 20 minutes

2 cups (500 ml) vegetable
  stock
5 fresh shiitake or other
  mushrooms, cut in half
¼ teaspoon sesame oil
¼ teaspoon salt
pinch of white sugar
pinch of white pepper
2 teaspoons nutritional yeast
2 drops yellow food coloring
  – optional
2½ tablespoons cornstarch
quarter 14-ounce (100 g)
  block extra-firm tofu,
  pressed (page 25) and
  grated
pinch of black salt
1 scallion, chopped

This traditional Chinese soup usually has wispy tendrils of egg suspended in it and is minimally seasoned. Here, grated firm tofu stands in for the egg – firm tofu holds its shape the best and won't leave your soup looking too lumpy, so I'd advise staying away from the silken sort.

Put the stock and mushrooms in a saucepan and bring to a boil, then stir in the sesame oil, salt, sugar, pepper, nutritional yeast and food coloring, if using.

In a small bowl whisk the cornstarch and 2½ tablespoons water with a fork until there are no lumps. Pour into the pan, stirring constantly, and continue to cook until the soup has thickened to a runny gravy-like consistency.

Stir in the grated tofu and black salt, then garnish with the scallion. Serve piping hot!

Black bean and mushroom stir-fry

Serves 2–3

—

Prep time: 20 minutes
Cooking time: 20 minutes

1 cup (210 g) sushi rice
¼ teaspoon salt
1 teaspoon vegetable oil
1 cm ginger, finely chopped
3 garlic cloves, finely chopped
1 tablespoon black bean paste
½ cup (90 g) baby corn, halved
½ cup (80 g) frozen edamame
1 cup (90 g) sliced mushrooms
1 cup (60 g) small broccoli florets
½ cup (125 ml) vegetable stock
1 teaspoon cornstarch
sliced scallions, to garnish

This dish was inspired by something my sister and I used to order at one of our favorite dim sum restaurants in London. The day they took it off the menu, my heart shattered like the caramel atop a crème brûlée – and I was forced to try and re-create it at home. A modern take on a Chinese stir-fry, juicy morsels of veg are stir-fried with a whisper of garlic. This is given a Japanese twist when spooned over a bed of sushi rice. Black bean paste is the key ingredient here, and you might come across different versions of it – some as a puree with garlic, some plain with whole beans – but you can use whatever you can find. Each will have a different intensity, so I recommend starting off with a tablespoon and tasting it to see if any more is needed.

Rinse the rice and drain. Continue to do this until the water runs clear – this usually takes 5–7 thorough rinses. Transfer the rice and 1¼ cups (310 ml) water into a saucepan that has a tight-fitting lid and add the salt. Bring to a boil over high heat, stirring constantly, then turn down the heat as low as possible, clamp on the lid and let the rice cook undisturbed for 15 minutes. Remove from the heat and leave the rice to sit for 10 minutes, without lifting the lid.

Meanwhile, heat the oil in a wok or nonstick frying pan over medium heat. Fry the ginger and garlic for 1–2 minutes, until fragrant. Add the black bean paste, baby corn, edamame, mushrooms and broccoli and stir well. Add the stock, then cover and cook until the corn and broccoli are tender, about 5 minutes.

In a small bowl, mix the cornstarch with 1 tablespoon plus 1 teaspoon water until smooth, then pour into the wok. Mix it in and cook, stirring constantly, until the liquid has thickened into a gravy-like sauce.

Serve the stir-fry over bowls of rice, garnished with sliced scallions.

"Thunder tea" rice

Serves 4
—

Prep time: 30 minutes
Cooking time: 45 minutes

Rice

1½ cups (300 g) long-grain
    brown rice
2¼ cups (560 ml) vegetable
    stock
2 teaspoons Chicken-style
    seasoning (page 20) – optional

Toppings

½ cup (70 g) whole raw peanuts
1 tablespoon plus 1 teaspoon
    vegetable oil
one 14-ounce (400 g) block
    extra-firm tofu, pressed (page
    25) and cubed
4 garlic cloves, finely chopped
2 heads bok choy (or other leafy
    greens), chopped
1 cup (125 g) chopped green
    beans
2 cups (180 g) shredded napa or
    savoy cabbage
1 cup (125 g) diced carrots

Green soup

1 teaspoon vegetable oil
2 cups (40 g) lightly packed Thai
    or regular basil leaves
2 cups (40 g) lightly packed mint
    leaves
1 cup (20 g) lightly packed
    cilantro leaves
⅓ cup (45 g) crushed peanuts
1 tablespoon plus 1 teaspoon
    sesame seeds
1 cup (250 ml) hot vegetable
    stock
1 inch (2.5 cm) ginger
½ teaspoon salt

This Hakka dish is supposed to detox your body, clear up your digestive system, and improve your complexion. While I don't subscribe to the idea of detoxes and cleanses, I really do adore this dish. The green soup, packed with brimming handfuls of fresh herbs, is a bit like an Asian pesto. You flood it over the fluffy rice and vegetables, then swirl everything together and eat up. While traditionally each topping is fried separately, you can stir-fry them all together to save time – just remember to start with the carrots and green beans first, before adding the quicker-cooking leafier veggies to the pan.

Place the rice, vegetable stock and chicken-style seasoning, if using, in a saucepan and bring to a boil. Lower the heat, cover and simmer until the rice is cooked through, about 30–45 minutes.

Meanwhile, fry the toppings. Dry-fry the peanuts in a nonstick frying pan over medium heat until golden and fragrant, then set aside. Add a little oil to the pan and fry the tofu cubes until golden and slightly crisp, then set aside. Add a little bit more oil and a quarter of the garlic and fry for about a minute, until aromatic. Next, add the bok choy and cook until just wilted, then set aside. Repeat with the green beans, cabbage and carrots, frying them all separately with a quarter of the garlic.

To make the soup, pour the rest of the oil into a large nonstick frying pan over medium heat and fry the basil, mint and cilantro leaves until they are beginning to wilt and soften, about 2–3 minutes. Add the peanuts and sesame seeds and keep frying to lightly toast them. When you start to smell the aroma of the peanuts, and the greens have wilted completely, remove from the heat and transfer the contents of the pan into a food processor or high-speed blender. Add the stock, ginger and salt and blend to a smooth puree.

To serve, spoon some brown rice onto a plate. Place a little bit of the fried tofu, bok choy, green beans, cabbage and carrot around the rice, then serve with a small bowl of green soup and some of the roasted peanuts alongside. Before eating, pour the soup over the rice and toss well.

Peking jackfruit pancakes

Makes 12 (enough for
4–6 as a starter)
—
Prep time: 30 minutes
Cooking time: 30 minutes

Pancake dough
1½ cups (225 g) all-purpose
  flour, sifted
pinch of salt
⅔ cup (170 ml) boiling water
1 tablespoon plus 1 teaspoon
  oil, for brushing

one 14-ounce (400 g) can
  young green jackfruit,
  prepared (page 25)
1 teaspoon sesame oil
1 inch (2.5 cm) ginger, finely
  chopped
2½ tablespoons rice wine,
  dry white wine or apple
  juice
½ teaspoon five spice powder
pinch of black pepper
1 tablespoon plus 1 teaspoon
  dark soy sauce
½ cup (100 g) hoisin sauce
  and thin strips of carrot,
  cucumber and scallion, to
  serve

I remember visiting a restaurant in Shanghai famed for its melt-in-your-mouth Peking duck and watching my parents deftly use chopsticks to pile shredded meat and crisp skin into the cradle of a paper-thin pancake. Duck pancakes have become a Chinese-restaurant classic and it is not difficult to see why. Dressed with fruity hoisin sauce and paired with fresh slivers of scallion for crunch, they are fun to assemble and eat. Young green jackfruit stands in for duck here – it can be shredded in much the same way and soaks up flavors beautifully. If you don't have time to make your own pancakes, feel free to use a dozen store-bought wheat spring roll wrappers.

First make the pancake dough. In a large bowl, knead the flour, salt and water until you have a smooth, elastic dough, about 5 minutes, adding a teaspoon more flour if it seems too sticky. Wrap the dough in plastic wrap and leave to rest for about 30 minutes.

Meanwhile, preheat the oven to 400°F (200°C). Place the shredded jackfruit in a loaf pan. Whisk together the sesame oil, ginger, wine, five spice, black pepper and soy sauce and pour over the jackfruit. Roast for 15–20 minutes or until very tender – there may still be liquid in the pan, and that's okay.

Unwrap the dough, roll it into a log and divide into twelve. Roll each piece of dough into a ball, then flatten slightly by patting it with the palm of your hand. Brush a thin layer of oil over six of the flattened dough balls, then place the un-oiled dough balls on top of them to form sandwiches. Use a rolling pin to roll out each sandwich into a flat pancake, flipping it midway so both sides are rolled evenly.

Set a dry nonstick frying pan over medium heat, place a pancake in it and cook until it is puffy and the bottom is flecked with brown, about 2–3 minutes. Flip it over and cook the other side for 2–3 minutes, then remove. Carefully separate the two layers to give you two pancakes. Keep on a plate, covered with a clean kitchen towel, while you cook the rest, separating them as well, to give you twelve in total.

Transfer the jackfruit to a serving platter. To eat, scoop a little bit of jackfruit onto a pancake, top with a drizzle of hoisin sauce and a few slivers of carrot, cucumber and scallion, then wrap up and enjoy.

Peanut meltaway cookies

Makes about 24 cookies
—

Prep time: 15 minutes
Cooking time: 15 minutes

1½ cups (200 g) roasted
  peanuts
⅔ cup (110 g) rice flour
⅔ cup (80 g) confectioners'
  sugar
½ teaspoon salt
⅓ cup plus 1 tablespoon
  (100 ml) peanut oil
2½ tablespoons soy milk
1 teaspoon agave syrup
handful of halved peanuts

These cookies are quick to make and, somewhat
unfortunately, they tend to disappear rather quickly as
well. They really do just melt away in your mouth! That's
why I like to make quite a large batch in one go. The
amount of oil you need will depend on the quality of your
rice flour and how oily your peanuts are, so add it gradually,
a little at a time, just until the dough holds together when
you squeeze it between your fingers. Adding too much oil
can make the cookies too delicate and crumbly.

Preheat the oven to 350°F (180°C) and line a large baking
sheet with parchment paper.

Pulse the peanuts in a food processor just until they
resemble sand. Do not overblend or you'll end up with
peanut butter! The best way to avoid this is to blend the
peanuts in 2–3 batches so that the nuts nearest the blade
don't get too finely ground.

Transfer the ground peanuts to a mixing bowl, sift in the
rice flour, sugar and salt and mix well. Slowly pour in the
oil, bit by bit, until the dough holds together when you
squeeze it between your fingers – you might not need to
use all the oil. Scoop out teaspoonfuls of the dough, roll
into balls and place on the baking sheet.

Make a glaze by stirring together the soy milk and agave
syrup. Place a peanut half on each cookie, brush with the
glaze and bake for 10–12 minutes, until golden. Let the
cookies cool for 5 minutes before removing from the sheet.

Mango pudding

Serves 6

—

Prep time: 15 minutes
Cooking time: 15 minutes

2 teaspoons agar powder
⅓ cup (75 g) white sugar
pinch of salt
1 cup (250 ml) coconut milk
1 cup (280 g) mango puree,
    from about 2 mangoes
1 teaspoon lime juice
chia seeds, coconut flakes
    and mint sprigs, to garnish

A favorite dessert in dim sum restaurants everywhere, this pudding is a promise of fruity, saccharine delight – ultra-creamy with just a tinge of tartness.

Put the agar into a saucepan with ½ cup (125 ml) water and bring to a boil, stirring constantly, then lower the heat and simmer for 3 minutes.

Meanwhile, place the sugar, salt, coconut milk, mango puree and lime juice in another pan and bring to a simmer.

Pour the mango mixture into the agar mixture and stir it in. As soon as it comes to a boil, take the mixture off the heat and pour into six ramekins or small bowls – do this carefully, so as not to create too many bubbles or splashes.

Chill for a minimum of 2 hours before serving, garnished with chia seeds, coconut flakes and mint sprigs.

Hong Kong "egg" tarts

 Use gluten-free puff pastry.

Makes 12
—

Prep time: 20 minutes
Cooking time: 15 minutes

1 sheet vegan puff pastry
one 12.3-ounce (349 g) block
    silken tofu, drained
½ cup (125 ml) soy milk
½ teaspoon vanilla extract
¼ cup (35 g) custard powder
    (or cornstarch plus more
    vanilla extract to taste and
    a pinch more salt)
½ cup (110 g) white sugar
pinch of salt

There was an egg tart shop right across the ribbon of road from my bus stop. I would sit there, slouched after a long day at school, and jump up when the glorious scent of baking pastry wafted over on the warm afternoon breeze. Then came the eternal debate: Would I have the time to dash across the street to buy one and still catch my bus? Layers of flaky, buttery pastry encased a custard just set enough not to flow out of the tart as you bit into it, but still yielding and velvety. These were tarts worth missing buses for. . . .

Preheat the oven to 450°F (230°C). Grease 12 disposable mini-tart pans or a 12-hole muffin pan.

Dust your work surface with flour and roll out the puff pastry into a 14 x 9-inch (35 x 23 cm) rectangle; prerolled sheets of pastry should have similar dimensions. Very lightly brush the sheet with water and then, with one of the shorter sides closest to you, fold over the edge of the pastry, tuck it in and start rolling up the sheet into a tight roll, as you would if you were making cinnamon rolls. Cut the roll of pastry into 12 slices. Take a slice and turn it over, so that the spiral you have formed is facing up. Use a rolling pin to roll it out into a circle about 5 mm thick. Place each pastry circle in a pan or muffin hole, pressing it down to fill the pan, then trim off any excess pastry around the edges.

To make the filling, put the tofu, soy milk, vanilla extract, custard powder, sugar and salt in a blender and blitz until smooth. Pour into a saucepan and bring to a boil over medium heat. Lower the heat and stir, until the custard thickens, about 2 minutes.

Pour the filling into the tart shells, then bake for 15 minutes, or until the pastry is golden and the custard is set but still has a slight wobble. These are best eaten when fresh, but if you have any left over, pop them in the oven for a few minutes so they're crisp and warm.

China

05
Japan

The first time I saw snow, I was in Japan. It was everywhere, like a glittering blanket of powdered sugar. It transformed the concrete jungle of Tokyo into something quite ethereal.

Going to Japan in the bitter depths of winter might not seem the smartest move. Why miss the chance to picnic under clouds of cherry blossoms in the springtime? Or in autumn, with the blazing copper of the turning leaves? But I was enchanted. Being cold – *really cold* – was a new feeling for me. *Winter*, I declared, *is my favorite season* . . . even though I would later discover how much I disliked it.

The Japanese are meticulous in all that they do. From intricately sculpted bonsai trees to platters of delicate sushi, their attention to detail is second to none. Nothing is ever noisy or flamboyant, and you soon find yourself filled with an almost overwhelming sense of calm and peace. Japan has mastered the complex art of simplicity, so much so that there is even a word for it: *shibui*. It is a word without a simple translation, although "subtle, simplistic beauty" comes close.

Tokyo is undeniably the world capital of fine dining, with more Michelin stars than any other city, beating even Paris: an impressive feat, for sure, but perhaps to be expected in a country that seeks perfection in all things. In the birthplace of umami, even street food surprises. From hearty noodle soups to custardy vegetable pancakes, everything may seem quite ordinary – until you sneak a taste. And another. And *another!* There is *always* more to Japan than meets the eye.

So, with your soy sauce bottle at the ready, cook your way through Japan. It would be a culinary crime not to. The hardest bit is deciding what to eat first.

Teriyaki tofu

(GF) *Use tamari in place of soy sauce.*

Serves 4

—

Prep time: 20 minutes (plus marinating time)

Cooking time: 30 minutes

one 14-ounce (400 g) block extra-firm tofu, pressed (page 25)

¼ cup (60 ml) light soy sauce

½ teaspoon ground ginger

¼ teaspoon garlic powder

¼ cup (45 g) lightly packed brown sugar

about ¼ cup (30 g) cornstarch

sliced scallion, red chili and sesame seeds, to serve

When I was younger, I would put teriyaki sauce on everything. It was my form of ketchup: the perfect condiment for almost every meal. While I no longer drown my food in it, one pairing that has stuck with me is teriyaki and crispy tofu. Although teriyaki sauce is readily available, homemade has even more flavor, and it is cheap and easy to make. Serve on a bed of steamed rice, sprinkled with a hefty dose of sesame seeds. This goes perfectly alongside Miso caramel eggplant (page 206).

First marinate the tofu. Cut the tofu into cubes. In a bowl, mix together the soy sauce, ginger, garlic, brown sugar and 1 cup (250 ml) water. Place the tofu cubes in the marinade, then cover and leave in the fridge for at least 1 hour.

Preheat the oven to 400°F (200°C) and line a baking sheet with parchment paper. Remove the tofu from the marinade, toss lightly in the cornstarch and place on the baking sheet. Bake the tofu for 25 minutes, flipping it over halfway through, until browned and crispy.

Meanwhile, place the remaining marinade in a saucepan. Mix 1 tablespoon plus 1 teaspoon cornstarch with ¼ cup (60 ml) water until smooth. Add to the pan and bring to a boil, then reduce the heat and simmer, stirring, until the sauce thickens.

Stir the crispy tofu cubes into the sauce and serve hot, garnished with scallion, chili and sesame seeds.

Baked tempura

Use gluten-free bread crumbs, and rice flour instead of wheat flour.

Serves 4 as a side
—
Prep time: 20 minutes
Cooking time: 15 minutes

1 sweet potato
1 eggplant
½ cup (60 g) green beans
5 ears baby corn
1 teaspoon vegetable oil
1 cup (60 g) panko bread crumbs
½ teaspoon salt
1 cup (150 g) all-purpose flour
pinch of cayenne pepper
pinch of ground turmeric
½ cup (125 ml) soy milk
2 teaspoons lemon juice

Dipping sauce
1 teaspoon white sugar
2½ tablespoons light soy sauce
1 dried shiitake mushroom
½ sheet nori, shredded
2½ tablespoons mirin

My sister is a tempura monster. She can single-handedly demolish a mountain of tempura prawns and still have room for more sushi and the mandatory post-meal mochi. I prefer *kakiage* – lengths of different vegetables encased in a tempura batter, drizzled with a sticky and sweet soy sauce. Here is my spin on vegetable tempura: I use panko bread crumbs, which may not be traditional but is a lovely way of adding crispiness without deep-frying. Frying the panko first gives them a lovely golden color – something that doesn't happen if you pop them into the oven straight from the package.

First prepare all the vegetables: Peel the sweet potato and cut into wedges 5 mm thick, then slice the eggplant into wedges 2 cm thick. Trim the green beans and slice each baby corn in half lengthwise.

Heat the oil in a large nonstick frying pan and fry the bread crumbs until they are evenly golden and crispy, then transfer to a wide, shallow bowl and season with half of the salt. Sift the flour into another bowl with the cayenne, turmeric and the rest of the salt, then toss well. In a third bowl, stir together the soy milk and lemon juice, then leave to sit and thicken for at least 5 minutes.

Preheat the oven to 450°F (230°C) and line a large baking sheet with parchment paper.

Dip each vegetable into the flour bowl, toss to coat, then shake off any excess and dip into the soy milk mixture. Finally, coat well with bread crumbs and place on the baking sheet.

When all the vegetables are coated, bake them for about 15 minutes, or until golden and fragrant.

Meanwhile, put all the dipping sauce ingredients except the mirin in a small saucepan. Add ½ cup (125 ml) water and bring to a boil, then remove from the heat and strain to remove the nori and shiitake mushroom. Pour the sauce into a small bowl and stir in the mirin.

Serve the tempura veggies with the dipping sauce on the side – and eat immediately, before the tempura loses its crunch.

Japanese curry

Use tamari instead of soy sauce, and rice flour instead of wheat flour.

Serves 4
—
Prep time: 25 minutes
Cooking time: 25 minutes

¼ cup (35 g) all-purpose flour

Japanese curry powder
2 tablespoons ground turmeric
1 tablespoon plus 1 teaspoon ground coriander
1 teaspoon ground cumin
½ teaspoon ground cardamom
½ teaspoon ground cinnamon
½ teaspoon ground ginger
¼ teaspoon cayenne pepper
¼ teaspoon ground cloves
¼ teaspoon ground nutmeg
¼ teaspoon five spice powder
¼ teaspoon black pepper

1 tablespoon plus 1 teaspoon vegetable oil
1 white onion, finely diced
1 garlic clove, finely chopped
2 large carrots, peeled and cubed
1 large potato, peeled and cubed
2½ tablespoons ketchup
2½ tablespoons Japanese curry powder (see above)
2½ cups (625 ml) vegetable stock
1 tablespoon plus 1 teaspoon sugar
2–3 teaspoons light soy sauce
1 Fuji apple, grated
½ cup (80 g) shelled edamame or fava beans
cooked short-grain rice, to serve
scallions and sesame seeds, to garnish

Japanese curries are sweeter and milder than Indian ones. Traditionally, they are made with a roux of flour, butter and a unique concoction of spices. This version skips the roux but gives a very similar result. I've included instructions for making your own curry powder below, but if you can find Japanese "oriental" curry powder, feel free to use that instead. Failing that, just use garam masala and a generous pinch of ground turmeric (most Indian curry powders will be too bold and spicy).

Preheat the oven to 400°F (200°C). Sift the flour onto a baking sheet and toast until brown, taking it out to give it a stir every 5 minutes or so – this should take about 20 minutes altogether. Leave to cool.

If you're making your own curry powder, simply mix together all the ingredients. (This makes more than you need here, but the rest can be stored in an airtight jar in your spice drawer for several months.)

Heat the oil in a large saucepan over medium heat and fry the onion and garlic until soft and translucent, 4–5 minutes. Add the carrots, potato, ketchup and 2½ tablespoons curry powder. Stir well and keep stir-frying for another 5 minutes, then add the stock. Bring to a boil, then simmer for about 10 minutes, until the vegetables are tender enough to pierce with a fork. Next add the sugar, soy sauce, grated apple and edamame and boil for another 2 minutes.

Scoop a ladle or two of the broth into a blender, pour in the toasted flour and blend until smooth and lump-free (you can also do this by hand – in a bowl with a whisk). Return the blended broth to the pan and simmer, stirring frequently, until thick and saucy, 5–10 minutes.

Serve the curry with rice, garnished with scallions and sesame seeds.

Omu-rice

GF — *Use tamari in place of soy sauce.*

Serves 2

—

Prep time: 20 minutes
Cooking time: 25 minutes

1 tablespoon plus 1 teaspoon
    vegetable oil
2 garlic cloves, finely chopped
1 cup (140 g) frozen mixed
    vegetables (corn, peas and
    diced carrot)
1½ cups (280 g) cooked
    short-grain rice, cooled
2½ tablespoons ketchup
1 teaspoon light soy sauce
¼ cup (20 g) TVP granules,
    prepared (page 25)
½ teaspoon salt
pinch of black pepper
1 teaspoon Chicken-style
    seasoning (page 20) or
    nutritional yeast
1 scallion, sliced

Omelet
half 12.3-ounce (349 g) block
    silken tofu
¼ cup (60 ml) soy milk
¼ cup (30 g) chickpea flour
¼ teaspoon salt
pinch of ground turmeric
1 teaspoon cornstarch
pinch of baking powder

black salt, ketchup and vegan
    mayonnaise, to serve
baby roma (plum) tomatoes,
    halved, and cilantro sprigs,
    to garnish

This Japanese version of fried rice is lavished with a delightfully wobbly vegan omelet. It's a delicious way to use up leftover rice and is usually a big hit with kids, especially when drizzled with glistening ribbons of ketchup and vegan mayo.

Pour the oil into a large wok or nonstick frying pan over medium heat and fry the garlic for 1 minute until fragrant, then add the mixed veg. Add ¼ cup (60 ml) water, cover and cook until all the vegetables are tender.

Add the rice and fry for a minute or so, using a wooden spoon or spatula to break apart any big clumps. Next, add the ketchup and soy sauce. Fry for 3–4 minutes, stirring to distribute the ketchup and soy sauce well. Add the drained TVP, salt and pepper, as well as the chicken-style seasoning. Mix well and fry for 2–3 minutes before taking it off the heat and garnishing with sliced scallion. Cover the pan to keep the fried rice warm while you make the omelet.

For the omelet, put all the ingredients in a blender and blitz to make a smooth, lump-free batter. Set a small nonstick frying pan over medium heat and pour half of the omelet mixture into the pan, swirling it around to cover the base of the pan. Cover and cook until the omelet is set and golden underneath, about 3–5 minutes, then flip and fry on the other side for a further 2–3 minutes. Repeat with the rest of the mixture to make a second omelet.

To serve, spoon some of the fried rice onto each plate and top with an omelet. Sprinkle with black salt and drizzle with ketchup and vegan mayonnaise. Garnish with tomato halves and a sprig of cilantro.

NOTE For a spin on this recipe, use Okonomiyaki sauce (page 205) instead of the ketchup in the rice and for drizzling over the omelet.

Summer chawanmushi

GF *Use tamari in place of soy sauce.*

Serves 2
—
Prep time: 10 minutes
Cooking time: 15 minutes

2 mushrooms, thinly sliced
½ small carrot, thinly sliced
1½ cups (375 ml) soy milk
1 teaspoon mirin
½ teaspoon light soy sauce
1 teaspoon nutritional yeast
½ teaspoon black salt
½ teaspoon white sugar
¼ teaspoon agar powder
¼ cup (40 g) cooked rice
   vermicelli noodles
1 scallion, sliced

Strewn with slivers of mushroom, gingko nuts, carrots and strands of vermicelli noodles, this savory egg custard is generally steamed in little cups. It can then be served hot or cold. This is my vegan version of chilled *chawanmushi* – usually eaten in the summer in Japan, when temperatures can soar. If you are making a meal of multiple courses, serve this *chawanmushi* as an interlude between two rich or complex dishes.

Bring a small saucepan of water to a boil, add the mushrooms and carrot and cook until the carrots are tender, about 3–4 minutes, then drain and set aside.

Rinse out the pan, then add the soy milk, mirin, soy sauce, nutritional yeast, salt and sugar. Mix to combine well, then add the agar powder and stir until it has completely dissolved. Set the pan over medium heat and bring to a boil, stirring constantly. Reduce to a simmer and cook for 3 minutes, still stirring constantly, then remove from the heat.

Divide the noodles between 2 Japanese teacups or small ramekins. Add half of the scallions and half of the mushroom and carrot mixture to each one, along with half of the heated soy milk mixture – do this carefully, so as not to create too many bubbles or splashes.

Chill in the fridge until set, about 1–2 hours, before serving.

Squash katsu-don

Use gluten-free bread crumbs, rice flour instead of wheat flour, and tamari instead of soy sauce.

Serves 2
—
Prep time: 30 minutes
Cooking time: 50 minutes

1 cup (150 g) cubed butternut or other winter squash
1 small shallot, finely diced
¼ teaspoon salt
pinch of white pepper
1 tablespoon plus 1 teaspoon all-purpose flour
¼ teaspoon white sugar
¼ cup (40 g) cooked sweet corn kernels

Onion dashi broth
1 cup (250 ml) Dashi (page 21) or vegetable stock
2½ tablespoons light soy sauce
2 teaspoons sugar
2½ tablespoons mirin
½ white onion, finely sliced

Panko coating
½ cup (30 g) panko bread crumbs
salt
2 tablespoons all-purpose flour
pinch of ground turmeric
pepper
¼ cup (60 ml) soy milk
1 teaspoon apple cider vinegar

cooked short-grain rice, to serve
sliced scallion, to garnish

A squash "cutlet" encased in a crisp golden shell perched on top of a bed of rice, all bathed in a sweet-and-salty broth with wilted onion. . . . It may sound rustic, but this *katsu-don* is a powerhouse of flavor. If you feel like jazzing it up a bit, add some scrambled tofu.

First, steam the squash cubes until they're tender enough to be easily pierced with a fork, about 20 minutes. Transfer into a large heatproof bowl and mash well, then stir in the diced shallot, salt, pepper, flour, sugar and corn kernels. Stir to mix everything thoroughly. Flatten the pumpkin mixture into two oval "cutlets," place on a baking sheet lined with parchment paper and leave in the freezer for 10–20 minutes to firm up.

Next, make the onion dashi broth. In a small saucepan, bring the dashi to a boil, then stir in the soy sauce, sugar, mirin and sliced onions. Reduce to a simmer, cover and cook until the onions are very soft, 7–10 minutes.

Preheat the oven to 450°F (230°C).

For the coating, dry-fry the panko bread crumbs in a nonstick frying pan until evenly golden. Place the toasted bread crumbs in a wide, shallow bowl and season with a pinch of salt. In another bowl, stir together the flour, turmeric and a pinch each of salt and pepper. In a third bowl, whisk together the soy milk and vinegar, then leave to sit for 5 minutes to thicken up slightly.

Take the baking sheet out of the freezer and place one of the squash cutlets in the flour mixture. Turn it gently to coat in a thin layer of flour all over, then dip into the soy milk mixture so the flour becomes tacky. Lastly, coat in the toasted bread crumbs, pressing the crumbs on to coat the cutlet completely. Return it to the baking sheet and repeat with the other cutlet, then bake the cutlets for 15 minutes.

To serve, divide the rice between two bowls, pour the onion dashi broth over it and top with the squash cutlets. Garnish with sliced scallion – and eat it while it's hot!

Shiitake "tonkotsu" ramen

Use gluten-free miso paste and tamari instead of soy sauce. You can use buckwheat or rice noodles in place of the wheat ones. Check that your liquid smoke is wheat-free (or use smoked paprika instead).

Serves 2

—

Prep time: 30 minutes
Cooking time: 40 minutes

"Tonkotsu" broth
1 teaspoon vegetable oil
2 garlic cloves, finely chopped
1 inch (2.5 cm) ginger, finely chopped
2 shallots, finely chopped
1 scallion, sliced
1 tablespoon plus 1 teaspoon sesame seeds
1 tablespoon plus 1 teaspoon miso paste
¼ cup (60 ml) hot water
1 recipe Dashi (page 21)
½ teaspoon sriracha
2 teaspoons nutritional yeast
¼ teaspoon salt
pinch of white pepper
½ teaspoon sesame oil
1 cup (250 ml) soy milk

2 nests (3.5 ounces/100 g) dried whole wheat noodles
1 teaspoon vegetable oil
1 cm ginger, finely chopped
1 scallion, sliced
1½ cups (100 g) sliced fresh shiitake mushrooms
2 teaspoons light soy sauce
1 teaspoon rice vinegar
1 teaspoon maple syrup
¼ teaspoon liquid smoke (or smoked paprika)

Toppings
sliced scallions
shredded nori
black and white sesame seeds
halved baby roma (plum) tomatoes
cooked edamame and sweet corn kernels

Hankering for a bowl of ramen, I decided to make a vegan version of the rich, marbled *tonkotsu* broth. The soup is usually stewed low and slow – in fact, very slow, often for 12 hours or longer. The result is a viscous liquid the color of buttermilk and absolutely bursting with umami. This plant-based version needs a much shorter cooking time and, once you've made the soup base, everything comes together in a jiffy. Use any of your favorite ramen toppings in place of those I've suggested.

First make the broth. Heat the oil in a large saucepan over medium heat and fry the garlic, ginger and shallots until the shallots are translucent, about 4 minutes. Stir in the scallion and sesame seeds and fry for another minute. In a small bowl, dissolve the miso paste in the hot water until smooth. Add this to the pan, along with the dashi. Bring to a boil, then carefully pour into a blender. Add the sriracha, nutritional yeast, salt, pepper and sesame oil, then blend until smooth. Return the broth to the saucepan and cover.

Cook your noodles according to the package instructions. Meanwhile, heat the oil in a nonstick frying pan over medium-high heat and fry the ginger and scallion until fragrant, about 2 minutes, stirring constantly to keep the ginger from burning. Add the mushrooms and fry until they begin to shrink, about 3 minutes. Pour in the soy sauce, vinegar, maple syrup and liquid smoke and bring to a boil, then simmer until the mushrooms are soft and caramelized, 5–7 minutes.

Just before you are ready to serve, bring your broth back to a boil. In a separate pan (or in the microwave) bring the soy milk to a boil, then pour it into the broth and stir well. (Heating the soy milk beforehand keeps it from curdling when it's added to the hot broth.)

To serve, divide the noodles and mushrooms between two bowls. Pour some broth into each bowl, then add your chosen toppings and eat immediately, while the soup is piping hot and the mushrooms are still warm.

Nigiri sushi

Makes 8 pieces of sushi
—
Prep time: 20 minutes (plus marinating time for red-pepper "salmon" and tofu "*tamago*" toppings)
Cooking time: 40 minutes

½ cup (105 g) sushi rice
¼ teaspoon salt
2 teaspoons rice vinegar or
    apple cider vinegar
1 teaspoon white sugar
sushi toppings
    (pages 198–199)
2 sheets nori
cucumber slices and halved
    cherry tomatoes, to garnish

The following are mix-and-match recipes, making enough rice and toppings for 8 nigiri sushi total. To make sushi for a crowd, start with four times the amount of rice and one quantity of each topping, giving you 32 pieces of sushi.

Rinse and drain the rice. Continue to do this until the water runs clear – this usually takes 5–7 thorough rinses. Transfer the rice and ⅔ cup (170 ml) water into a saucepan that has a tight-fitting lid and add the salt. Bring to a boil over high heat, stirring constantly, then turn down the heat as low as possible, clamp on the lid and let the rice cook undisturbed for 15 minutes. Remove from the heat and leave the rice to sit for 10 more minutes, without lifting the lid.

Meanwhile, mix together the vinegar and sugar until the sugar has dissolved.

Now take the lid off the rice and stir it around with a rice paddle or wooden spatula. Use a paper fan, or a book, to fan the rice and cool it down more quickly, gradually pouring in the vinegar mixture and stirring to mix well. Go gently so as not to break up the rice too much.

When the rice is at room temperature, divide it into eight balls, then shape each ball into a sushi-sized log about 2 inches (5 cm) in length. Top with your chosen toppings, wrap with nori and serve garnished with cucumber and tomato.

Red-pepper "salmon" sushi topping

Make sure the liquid smoke does not contain wheat (or use smoked paprika instead).

Makes enough for 8 pieces of sushi

1 red bell pepper
1 teaspoon liquid smoke
(or ½ teaspoon smoked paprika)
½ teaspoon apple cider vinegar
1 tablespoon plus 1 teaspoon vegetable oil
¼ teaspoon salt

Pierce the pepper all over with the tip of a small knife, then broil until black and blistered, turning it every 5 minutes – this should take 15–20 minutes. Use a fork to whisk together the liquid smoke, vinegar, oil and salt in a bowl.

When the pepper is blackened, plunge it into a bowl of cold water and leave for a minute or so to loosen the skin.

Remove the pepper and peel off the skin, then cut the pepper in half lengthwise and remove the stem and seeds. Slice each pepper half into four lengthwise, giving you eight slices of pepper.

Add the pepper slices to the bowl of marinade and leave in the fridge to marinate for at least half an hour – they taste better the longer you leave them!

To assemble, place a slice of pepper on top of a rice log, cut thin strips of nori and wrap it around the sushi, using a bit of water to make the nori stick to itself and seal.

Tofu "tamago" sushi topping

Makes enough for 8 pieces of sushi

Half 14-ounce (400 g) block extra-firm tofu, pressed (page 25)
¼ cup (60 ml) plant milk
¼ teaspoon ground turmeric
1 teaspoon nutritional yeast
pinch of black salt

Slice the tofu lengthwise into four long pieces, then cut each piece into two, giving you eight shorter rectangles in total. In a wide shallow bowl, mix together the milk, turmeric, nutritional yeast and salt. Lay the tofu in the bowl in a single layer, then leave to marinate in the fridge for 20 minutes, flipping the pieces over halfway.

To assemble, place a piece of tofu on top of a rice log, cut thin strips of nori and wrap around the sushi, using a dab of water to make the nori stick to itself and seal.

Edamame sushi topping

**Makes enough for 8 pieces
of sushi**

½ cup (80 g) frozen
    edamame
½ teaspoon lemon juice
pinch of salt
white sesame seeds, for
    sprinkling

Cook the edamame in a small saucepan of boiling water until tender, then toss in the lemon juice and salt. To assemble, cut the nori into thick strips, cutting along the natural indentations in the sheet. Wrap a strip around each rice log, using a dab of water to seal the ends of the nori. Scoop some edamame into the little pocket created between the top of the nori and the rice, then sprinkle with sesame seeds.

Eggplant "unagi" sushi topping

 *Use tamari instead
of soy sauce.*

**Makes enough for 8 pieces
of sushi**

1 small eggplant
2½ tablespoons light soy
    sauce
2½ tablespoons mirin
1 tablespoon plus 1 teaspoon
    white sugar
1 tablespoon plus 1 teaspoon
    dry white wine

Pierce the eggplant all over with the tip of a small knife, then broil until black and blistered, turning it every 5 minutes – this should take 15–20 minutes.

Meanwhile, to make a glaze for the eggplant, put the soy sauce, mirin, sugar and wine in a small saucepan and bring to a boil. Simmer, uncovered, for about 5 minutes, until the glaze is thick and syrup-like. Set aside.

Preheat the oven to 350°F (180°C) and lightly grease a baking sheet.

When the eggplant is blackened, plunge it into a bowl of cold water and leave for a minute or so to loosen the skin.

Remove the eggplant and peel off the skin, then gently trim away the top – take care as the eggplant will be very tender and you do not want to tear it. Cut the eggplant lengthwise into eight rectangular pieces roughly the same size as the logs of sushi rice.

Place the eggplant pieces on the baking sheet and brush with a third of the glaze. Bake for 3 minutes, then remove and brush with another third of the glaze. Repeat once more, so the eggplant is glazed three times and baked for 9 minutes in total.

To assemble, place each wedge of glazed eggplant on top of a rice log. Cut thin strips of nori and wrap it around the sushi, using a dab of water to make the nori stick to itself and seal.

Onigiri

Use tamari instead of soy sauce.

Makes 3 rice balls (enough for 1 as a main or 3 as a side)
—
Prep time: 20 minutes
Cooking time: 25 minutes

½ cup (105 g) sushi rice
pinch of salt
2 teaspoons white sesame
  seeds
2 teaspoons black sesame
  seeds

Filling
1 teaspoon vegetable oil
1 garlic clove, finely chopped
1 cup (60 g) sliced fresh
  shiitake mushrooms
¼ cup (40 g) frozen
  edamame
1 tablespoon plus 1 teaspoon
  light soy sauce
1 teaspoon agave syrup
1 teaspoon yuzu juice (or
  orange juice)
1 teaspoon cornstarch

1 sheet nori

These stuffed rice pyramids are the perfect thing for a packed lunch, and my version has a zesty teriyaki-drenched filling. If you're planning to eat these later, pack the nori separately and use it to wrap the onigiri just before you eat them. Otherwise, the nori will get soggy from being nestled up against the rice for too long.

Rinse and drain the rice. Continue to do this until the water runs clear – this usually takes 5–7 thorough rinses. Transfer the rice and ⅔ cup (170 ml) water into a saucepan that has a tight-fitting lid and add the salt. Bring to a boil over high heat, stirring constantly, then turn down the heat as low as possible, clamp the lid on the pan and let the rice cook undisturbed for 15 minutes. Remove from the heat and leave the rice to sit for 10 minutes, without lifting the lid.

Now take the lid off the rice and stir it around with a rice paddle or wooden spatula. Use a paper fan, or a book, to fan the rice and cool it down more quickly, gradually sprinkling in the sesame seeds and stirring to mix well. Go gently so as not to break up the rice too much.

To make the filling, heat the oil in a nonstick frying pan over medium heat. Fry the garlic for a minute until fragrant, then add the mushrooms and let them cook, without stirring, until they shrink to about a third of their original size. Add the edamame to the pan, as well as the soy sauce, agave and yuzu. In a small bowl, mix the cornstarch with 1 tablespoon plus 1 teaspoon water until no lumps remain, then pour into the pan. Quickly stir it in and cook, stirring constantly, until the sauce thickens. Leave the filling to cool.

To help with shaping the rice balls, tear off a large sheet of plastic wrap. With the wrap laid over the palm of your hand, scoop about a sixth of the rice into it. Use your other hand to flatten the rice into a circle, then form a dip in the center of the rice by curving your palm to create a bowl-like shape. Scoop in some of the filling, then add another sixth of the rice on top, covering the filling completely. Fold the plastic wrap up and around it and shape the rice ball into a pyramid. Repeat to form the other two onigiri.

Cut strips of nori and wrap around the base of each onigiri – this helps you hold them as you eat, as the rice is sticky!

Okonomiyaki

Serves 2

—

Prep time: 20 minutes
Cooking time: 20 minutes

Okonomiyaki sauce
2½ tablespoons ketchup
1 tablespoon plus 1 teaspoon
  barbecue sauce
1 teaspoon light soy sauce

¾ cup (100 g) all-purpose
  flour
¼ cup (30 g) chickpea flour
1 tablespoon plus 1 teaspoon
  nutritional yeast
½ teaspoon baking powder
¼ teaspoon black salt
1 cup (250 ml) vegetable
  stock
1½ cups (120 g) shredded
  napa cabbage, savoy
  cabbage or kale, any tough
  stalks removed
⅓ cup (50 g) lightly packed
  grated carrot
2 scallions, chopped
oil, for brushing
vegan mayo, sesame seeds,
  shredded nori and sliced
  scallion, to garnish
pickled ginger, to serve

Okonomiyaki means "as you like it," and that pretty much sums up this savory pancake. You can stir in a whole melange of shredded vegetables, but my favorite combination is napa cabbage, carrot for subtle sweetness, and scallions to perk it all up. Take care not to overmix the batter, as this makes for a rather tough okonomiyaki. Just fold until the vegetables are well coated with batter and then pour into a hot frying pan. You want your okonomiyaki to be still slightly custardy in the middle, so don't overcook it either!

For the okonomiyaki sauce, stir all the ingredients together and store in the fridge until needed – it will keep for up to a month.

Sift both flours, the yeast, baking powder and salt into a large bowl. Add the stock and mix to form a batter. Fold in the vegetables until just combined, being careful not to overwork the batter.

Heat a nonstick skillet or small frying pan and brush with oil. Pour half of the batter into the hot pan and cook for 6–10 minutes before flipping and cooking on the other side for 4–7 minutes. When it's done, the okonomiyaki should be golden on both sides but still have a slight jiggle in the center. Make a second one with the remaining batter.

Top each okonomiyaki with okonomiyaki sauce, then drizzle with vegan mayo and sprinkle with a good handful of sesame seeds, shredded nori and sliced scallion. Eat warm, with pickled ginger on the side.

Miso caramel eggplant

Use gluten-free miso paste.

Serves 4–6 as a side
—
Prep time: 15 minutes (plus marinating time)
Cooking time: 40 minutes

4 eggplants
¼ cup (70 g) miso paste
2 teaspoons sesame oil
¼ cup (60 ml) maple syrup
¼ cup (60 ml) warm water
1 cm ginger, finely chopped
½ teaspoon garlic powder
1 tablespoon plus 1 teaspoon
  black sesame seeds
1 tablespoon plus 1 teaspoon
  white sesame seeds
sliced scallion and red chili,
  to garnish

Eggplant is a fickle beast. It can sometimes be bitter, but if treated the right way it absorbs flavors like a sponge. This dish is part of my ongoing campaign to earn the eggplant some well-deserved glory – and *nasu dengaku* is good enough to sway any eggplant-hater! Let your spoon shatter the caramelized sesame "crust" and sink into tender, melting eggplant flesh....

Cut the eggplants in half lengthwise, then score each eggplant half with a diamond pattern, making sure not to cut right through to the skin.

In a bowl, whisk together the miso, sesame oil, maple syrup, warm water, ginger and garlic powder to make a marinade. Pour into a roasting pan and lay the eggplants, scored side down, in the marinade. Leave to marinate for 1–2 hours.

Preheat the oven to 400°F (200°C). Cover the roasting pan with foil and bake the eggplants for 30–35 minutes, until very tender. Remove from the oven, take off the foil and flip the eggplants over, then spoon some of the cooking juices from the pan over the eggplants. Sprinkle with a generous layer of sesame seeds, then return to the oven, uncovered, for another 5 minutes to toast the sesame seeds and give them a lovely crunch.

Serve garnished with scallion and chili slices. If you like, you can pour any remaining cooking juices into a small bowl and serve alongside the eggplant.

Yaki soba stir-fry

Use tamari instead of soy sauce, and a gluten-free hoisin sauce. Make sure your soba noodles are 100 percent buckwheat, as many contain wheat; health-food shops often have more to choose from.

Serves 4

—

Prep time: 20 minutes
Cooking time: 20 minutes

Yaki soba sauce
2 teaspoons light soy sauce
2 teaspoons hoisin sauce
½ teaspoon lemon juice
½ teaspoon sriracha
1 teaspoon ketchup

7 ounces (200 g) dried soba noodles (about 2 bundles)
1 tablespoon plus 1 teaspoon vegetable oil
2 garlic cloves, finely chopped
1 scallion, sliced
1 carrot, peeled and sliced
1 cup (60 g) small broccoli florets
1 cup (90 g) sliced mushrooms
½ cup (80 g) frozen edamame
black and white sesame seeds, to serve

Somewhat confusingly, the noodles used in a traditional *yaki soba* are closer to ramen noodles than they are to buckwheat-based soba. But, since I am partial to the earthiness of soba noodles, that is what I have used for my version. The eagle-eyed among you may also have noticed the addition of hoisin sauce, which is more of a Chinese ingredient than a Japanese one, but here it flavors the tangle of noodles with the barbecue-like taste that is characteristic of a good yaki soba.

For the yaki soba sauce, simply mix all the ingredients in a small bowl.

In a small saucepan, cook the soba noodles according to the instructions on the package. Drain, then dunk the noodles into a bowl of cold water and set aside.

Pour the oil into a large nonstick frying pan or wok over medium-high heat and fry the garlic and scallion until fragrant, then add the carrot slices and broccoli. Add ¼ cup (60 ml) water, cover and cook for 4–5 minutes, until the veggies are soft. Stir in the mushrooms and edamame and cook for another 2 minutes, or until the mushrooms shrink and soften.

Drain the noodles and add to the pan, then pour in the yaki soba sauce. Stir to mix everything well, then cook for 1–2 minutes, just to heat up the noodles. Scatter with the sesame seeds and serve immediately.

Spicy tomato "tuna" hand rolls

GF — Use tamari instead of soy sauce.

Makes 8 (enough for 2 as a main)

—

Prep time: 25 minutes (plus marinating time)
Cooking time: 20 minutes

4 tomatoes

Marinade
2 teaspoons light soy sauce
1–2 tablespoons sriracha, depending on how spicy you like it
2 teaspoons vegan mayonnaise
1 teaspoon sesame oil
2 teaspoons toasted sesame seeds
2 scallions, chopped
¼ teaspoon salt

⅔ cup (140 g) sushi rice
¼ teaspoon salt
2 teaspoons rice vinegar or apple cider vinegar
1 teaspoon white sugar
4 sheets nori, cut into half
½ small cucumber, cut into thin strips
black and white sesame seeds, to serve

While the tomato here isn't going to hoodwink a sushi enthusiast, the blanching completely transforms its texture, and the marinade gives it a more mellow flavor. The result is a fresh take on spicy tuna hand rolls.

Bring a large saucepan of water to a boil. Score a shallow "X" in the base of each tomato, then pop them into the boiling water, immersing them completely. Leave for 40–60 seconds, then carefully remove with a pair of tongs and immediately plunge them into a large bowl of cold water. Leave them for a minute or so, until the skin starts to peel away, then drain and peel off the skins – they should come away quite easily. Cut each tomato into quarters, scoop out and discard the seeds, then chop the tomato flesh into small chunks.

For the marinade, mix together all the ingredients in a bowl. Add the tomato chunks and toss to coat well, then cover and marinate in the fridge for at least 1 hour – the longer you leave them, the better the flavor.

Rinse and drain the rice. Continue to do this until the water runs clear – this usually takes 5–7 thorough rinses. Transfer the rice and a generous ¾ cup (200 ml) water into a saucepan that has a tight-fitting lid and add the salt. Bring to a boil over high heat, stirring constantly, then turn down the heat as low as possible, clamp on the lid and let the rice cook undisturbed for 15 minutes. Remove from the heat and leave the rice to sit for 10 minutes, without lifting the lid.

Meanwhile, mix together the vinegar and sugar until the sugar has dissolved.

Now take the lid off the rice and stir it around with a rice paddle or wooden spatula. Use a paper fan, or a book, to fan the rice and cool it down more quickly, gradually pouring in the vinegar mixture and stirring to mix well. Go gently so as not to break up the rice too much.

When the rice is cool enough to handle, lay a piece of nori on the countertop, with the matte side facing up. Follow the diagrams opposite to fill your hand rolls with cucumber strips and the marinated tomatoes, shaking off any excess marinade. Sprinkle with sesame seeds and serve.

How to make hand rolls

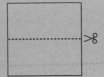

Cut the nori sheet in half.

Spread a thin layer of rice to one side of the nori.

Lay your fillings, such as cucumber, spicy tomato and sesame seeds, on the rice.

Start to roll the bottom corner up to form a cone.

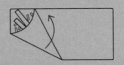

Continue to roll, wrapping the rest of the nori around the cone.

Use a few grains of rice to seal the nori to itself.

Red bean pancakes

Makes about 12

—

Prep time: 15 minutes
Cooking time: 1 hour

1 cup (250 ml) plant milk

¼ cup (55 g) white sugar

1 tablespoon plus 1 teaspoon
rice syrup

¼ teaspoon salt

1 tablespoon baking powder

1 tablespoon plus 1 teaspoon
vegetable oil, plus extra for
frying

1 cup (150 g) all-purpose
flour

1 recipe Red bean paste
(page 22) or 13 ounces
(375 g) store-bought red
bean paste

These little, round, bronze pancake sandwiches called *dorayaki* are normally brimming with red bean paste. The paste itself is made from maroon adzuki beans boiled with sugar and then mashed into a silky puree. If you are not a fan of red bean paste, these pancakes can also be stuffed with a vegan chocolate spread.

In a large bowl, mix together the plant milk, sugar, syrup, salt, baking powder and oil. Sift in the flour and fold in gently until just combined.

Heat a large nonstick frying pan over medium heat and add a little oil, wiping out any excess with a paper towel. Drop about 2 tablespoons batter into the pan and use a spatula to shape it into a small circle about 3 inches (8 cm) in diameter. If you have a large enough pan, you should be able to cook two or three pancakes at a time. Fry for 2–3 minutes, until bubbles form in the batter without bursting, then flip over and fry on the other side for 2–3 minutes. When the pancakes are done, both sides should be a lovely golden brown.

To assemble, scoop a heaped tablespoon of red bean filling onto a pancake, then top with another pancake. You should end up with about 12 pancake sandwiches in all.

Strawberry mochi

 Makes 10
—

Prep time: 20 minutes
Cooking time: 15 minutes

¾ cup (100 g) glutinous rice
   flour
¼ cup (55 g) white sugar
1 teaspoon matcha powder –
   optional
½ cup (60 g) cornstarch, plus
   extra for dusting
10 strawberries, hulled
1 recipe Red bean paste
   (page 22) or 13 ounces
   (375 g) store-bought red
   bean paste

Biting into one of these is a sensory journey: first the chewy skin of the mochi, then the velvety red bean paste and finally the fresh, juicy strawberry flesh.
You can, of course, use whatever fruit you prefer. The matcha adds a lovely bitter note that complements the sweetness of the red bean paste and strawberries, but you can leave it out if you don't have any.

In a heatproof bowl that will fit inside your steamer basket, whisk the glutinous rice flour, sugar and matcha with ¾ cup (185 ml) water until you have a smooth, lump-free batter. Place the bowl of mochi batter in the steamer basket, set it over a pan of boiling water and steam for 15 minutes, giving it a stir halfway through.

Dust the countertop with some of the cornstarch and rub some over your rolling pin. Pour the steamed mochi out of the bowl onto the counter, taking care not to burn yourself, as it will be very hot. Dust the mochi with cornstarch and slowly roll it out into a 5 mm thick sheet, dusting with more cornstarch as necessary. Leave to cool for 10–15 minutes.

Meanwhile, use your hands to roll the red bean paste into 10 balls. Working with one at a time, flatten it out in the palm of your hand, place a strawberry on top and bring the bean paste up around it, to encase the strawberry. Set aside.

Using a cookie cutter (3–4 inches/8–10 cm in diameter, depending on the size of your strawberries), cut out circles of mochi dough. Set a bean-paste-covered strawberry on each mochi circle and bring the dough up to cover it entirely, pinching the top to seal.

Place the finished mochi in cupcake liners to keep them from sticking together. Any not eaten right away can be kept in the fridge for up to a week.

Chocolate custard matcha buns

Makes 8

—

Prep time: 30 minutes (plus proofing and setting time)
Cooking time: 30 minutes

½ cup (125 ml) lukewarm plant milk
¼ cup plus 1 tablespoon (70 g) white sugar
1 packet (2½ teaspoons) active dry yeast
¼ cup (70 g) vegan yogurt or coconut milk
¼ cup (60 ml) aquafaba (page 11)
1 tablespoon plus 1 teaspoon vegetable oil
2½ cups (300 g) sifted all-purpose flour
¼ teaspoon salt
1½ teaspoons matcha powder

Chocolate custard
scant 1¼ cups (300 ml) soy milk
2 tablespoons custard powder (or cornstarch plus more vanilla extract to taste and a pinch more salt)
¼ cup (55 g) white sugar
2 teaspoons cocoa powder
pinch of salt
½ teaspoon vanilla paste or 1 teaspoon vanilla extract
1 tablespoon plus 1 teaspoon finely grated orange zest – optional

white sesame seeds, for coating

These are the perfect sweet treat for days when it's too hot to turn on the oven. The buns are scorched in a frying pan, so they get caramelized and crisp on the outside, then burst with molten chocolate goo when you tear into them.

In a large bowl or the bowl of a stand mixer, stir together the warm milk, sugar and yeast. Leave for 5 minutes, or until frothy, then stir in the yogurt, aquafaba and oil. Add the flour, salt and matcha and mix well.

Now knead the dough, either by using the dough hook attachment of the stand mixer or by hand, pouring the dough out onto a well-floured countertop. It is ready when it's smooth and elastic – this should take 7–10 minutes of kneading. Shape it into a ball and put it back in the bowl, then cover with a clean kitchen towel and leave somewhere warm to rise until it has doubled in size, about an hour.

Meanwhile, make the chocolate custard. Put all the ingredients in a saucepan and mix together until no lumps remain. Set the pan over medium heat and bring to a boil, stirring constantly. Lower the heat and let it simmer for 10 minutes, still stirring constantly, so the custard thickens evenly and doesn't become lumpy. Pour the custard into a heatproof bowl and chill in the fridge for at least an hour, or until set.

Punch the risen dough down, to knock out some of the air, then pour out onto a floured countertop and divide into eight. Use a rolling pin to roll out each ball into an oval about 5 x 3 inches (13 x 7.5 cm). Take the custard from the fridge and dollop a generous tablespoonful in the middle, then fold the dough over the custard, pinching the edges together firmly to seal well. Pat down gently to flatten the buns and spread the filling. Once all the buns are filled, set them aside for 5–10 minutes, until lightly puffed. Coat both sides of the buns with sesame seeds, pressing them onto the surface.

To cook, heat a large nonstick frying pan (with a lid) over medium heat and fit 2–3 buns in the pan, leaving a bit of space in between for them to expand as they cook. Cover and cook for 5–6 minutes, until the bottoms of the buns are golden brown and crisp. Flip them over and cook for 5–6 minutes on the other side.

These buns are best served warm, so the custard oozes out when you take a bite!

Mix-and-match leftovers

As you cook your way through this book, you will have leftovers, such as extra red bean paste from the mochi recipe, or spare bao dough. This is inevitable, as vegetables such as cauliflowers vary in size and sometimes – okay, most of the time – we snack along the way. So, what are you supposed to do with all that Peking jackfruit now you've run out of pancakes?

Enter the "mix-and-match" page. What I love about these recipes is how well they go together, and how flexible they are. This is by no means an exhaustive list of all the ways you can use up these odds and ends, just some combinations that I have found work well together. It's also a great resource if you feel like swapping around a recipe even before you make it.

If you don't see a particular dish, do read through the whole list, as it might be listed as a swap for something else!

Gua bao with sweet potato "belly" (page 156)
Spare buns: Fill with Peking jackfruit (page 172), Sweet and sour mushrooms (page 153) or the Lettuce cup filling (page 162).

Spare bun dough: Make filled buns, stuffing them with "Char siew" (page 124), Red bean paste (page 22) or Chocolate custard (page 216).

Spicy tomato "tuna" hand rolls (page 210)
Spare rice: Make hand rolls filled with Eggplant "unagi" (page 199) or Baked tempura (page 185).

Onigiri (page 202)
Spare rice: Stuff with some filling leftover from Spicy tomato "tuna" hand-rolls (page 210) or Lettuce cups (page 162), or use chopped-up Baked tempura (page 185) or Peking jackfruit (page 172).

Strawberry mochi (page 215)
Spare mochi skin: Use to wrap small scoops of your favorite vegan ice cream.

Squash katsu-don (page 192)
Mix it up: Instead of the Onion dashi broth, make some Japanese curry (page 187) to pour over the rice. For extra protein, add a vegan "omelet" (page 188) to top the rice.

Spare rice: top with Baked tempura (page 185) instead of the squash "cutlet."

Fluffy peanut pancake (page 104)
Spare pancake: Slather with some Coconut kaya custard (page 136) instead of the sweet peanut mixture.

Red bean pancakes (page 212)
Spare pancakes: Fill with Coconut kaya custard (page 136), crunchy peanut butter, or Chocolate custard (page 216).

Peking jackfruit pancakes (page 172)
Spare pancakes: Roll around the filling from
Gua bao with sweet potato "belly" (page 156) or
Popiah spring rolls (page 112).

Satay (page 103)
Spare sauce: Use as a dressing for Malaysian
rojak salad (page 111) instead of the hoisin
dressing. Or, use as a dipping sauce for Popiah
spring rolls (page 112). You can also serve this
sauce with "Thunder tea" rice (page 171), in place
of the green soup.

Hong Kong "egg" tarts (page 178)
Spare pastry shells: Use Coconut kaya custard
(page 136) as a filling instead of the custard, then
bake in the same way.

Vegan roti John (page 127)
Mix it up: Drizzle with Sambal (page 121) instead
of sriracha – or, for something totally different,
try using Satay sauce (page 103).

Rice noodle rolls (page 145)
Mix it up: Just before rolling up the steamed
batter, finely chop some vegan "Char siew" filling
(page 124) and sprinkle it over. Roll up, then serve
with light soy sauce instead of hoisin sauce.

Teriyaki tofu (page 182)
Spare sauce: Use it to top your Okonomiyaki
(page 205) or Omu-rice (page 188) in place of
ketchup.

Omu-rice (page 188)
Mix it up: Ditch the "omelet" and use some
Sambal (page 121) instead of the ketchup when
frying the rice to turn this into Malaysian *nasi
goreng*.

Pandan waffles (page 135)
Mix it up: Fill with Coconut kaya custard
(page 136) instead of peanut butter.

Hainanese "chicken" rice (page 118)
Spare roasted Seitan "chicken": Chop up and use
to fill Onigiri (page 202), or add to Tofu pad thai
(page 72). You could also use this as a filling for
Gua bao (page 156).

Cauliflower samosas (page 29)
Spare filling: Use it as a filling in your Dosas
(page 39) for something more like masala dosas.

Dumpling noodles (page 165)
Mix it up: Add some vegan "Char siew" (page 124)
to the noodles.

Scallion pancakes (page 150)
Mix it up: Fill the pancakes with some Peking
jackfruit (page 172) and make little sandwiches
out of them.

Mango summer rolls (page 80)
Mix it up: Instead of mango and mint, fill the rolls
with Peking jackfruit (page 172) and slivers
of cucumber.

Index

Thank you

Writing a book was not what I imagined it to be. It's a lot of work, a lot of cooking, and (rather fortunately) a lot of eating. I had a blast, but it wouldn't have been half as fantastic without some pretty cool people. It takes a village to write a cookbook – and it certainly takes a village to finish up all the leftovers.

Kyra: First, and always first, thank you to my amazing baby sister and hand model extraordinaire. No one holds a bowl with as much elegance as you. I love cooking for you, even though I don't get to do it very often anymore. Hopefully this book will give you a little help while trying to feed yourself down under. Nutrigrain is a tasty snack, but not a proper dinner – remember that. I miss you infinitely.

Shree: I think it goes without saying that I wouldn't be here without you. This year was incredibly tough but you made it so so much better. You are the only person I know who loves cardamom as much as I do – whenever I cook halwa or kulfi I remember that Easter when we discovered we could buy ground cardamom in the bulk bin section of Whole Foods. I miss our regular (perhaps too regular!) trips there, and getting cross at the salad bar whenever the teriyaki tofu was MIA. And, hey, now we can make our own!

Alex: Thank you so much for always believing in me, even when I didn't. No one else fights me for the washing up (hint: if you want to win, hide the sponge), or never gets tired of eating sweet chili jam (which, while in this situation is a blessing, can also be a curse). Without you, there would be no book. And, even if there was, everything would be way too spicy.

My family: For teaching me all that I know and for turning me into the little foodie that I am. You have helped shape the way this book has turned out, from lending me old lace doilies and tarnished trays, to helping brainstorm ways to take the chicken out of chicken rice. No one makes a feast quite like you do, and that made testing 3–4 recipes a day a lot less daunting.

My agent, Jane, and the incredible teams at Murdoch and The Experiment: You helped me turn my idea into a gorgeous book. Never in my wildest dreams had I imagined getting the chance to do something this cool. You were there every step of the way, so thank you for believing in me and letting me write my dream book.

The Humes: Thank you so much for letting me turn your beautiful kitchen into an absolute mess, and for being such willing taste-testers. Sorry for using up all your soy sauce! x

My readers: My virtual family – nothing would have been possible if I didn't have anyone to write this cookbook for. So, thank you for all the support, feedback and heart emojis. I hope you love this book as much as I have loved writing it.

EAST MEETS VEGAN: *The Best of Asian Home Cooking, Plant-Based and Delicious*
Text and photography copyright © 2019 by Sasha Gill

Originally published in the UK as *Jackfruit & Blue Ginger* by Murdoch Books, an imprint of Allen & Unwin, in 2019. First published in North America in revised form by The Experiment, LLC, in 2019.

The Experiment, LLC
220 East 23rd Street, Suite 600 | New York, NY 10010-4658
theexperimentpublishing.com

THE EXPERIMENT and its colophon are registered trademarks of The Experiment, LLC. Many of the designations used by manufacturers and sellers to distinguish their products are claimed as trademarks. Where those designations appear in this book and The Experiment was aware of a trademark claim, the designations have been capitalized.

The Experiment's books are available at special discounts when purchased in bulk for premiums and sales promotions as well as for fund-raising or educational use. For details, contact us at info@theexperimentpublishing.com.

Library of Congress Cataloging-in-Publication Data

Names: Gill, Sasha, author.
Title: East meets vegan : the best of asian home cooking, plant-based and delicious / Sasha Gill.
Other titles: Jackfruit and blue ginger
Description: New York, NY : The Experiment, 2019. | "Published as Jackfruit and Blue Ginger in the UK, Australia, and New Zealand by Murdoch Books in 2019." | "Ninety affordable, delicious vegan recipes that capture the color, spice and flavor of dishes from six Asian countries: India, Thailand, Singapore, Malaysia, China, and Japan."--Publisher. | Includes bibliographical references and index.
Identifiers: LCCN 2018043596 (print) | LCCN 2018044774 (ebook) | ISBN 9781615195640 (ebook) | ISBN 9781615195633 (pbk.)
Subjects: LCSH: Vegetarian cooking--Asia. | Cooking, Asian. | LCGFT: Cookbooks.
Classification: LCC TX837 (ebook) | LCC TX837 .G556 2019 (print) | DDC 641.5/6362095--dc 3
LC record available at https://lccn.loc.gov/2018043596

ISBN 978-1-61519-563-3
Ebook ISBN 978-1-61519-564-0

Cover design by Beth Bugler
Author photograph copyright © 2019 by Steve Brown
Design copyright © 2019 by Murdoch Books

Manufactured in China

First printing March 2019
10 9 8 7 6 5 4 3